RIDGELY TORRENCE
by John M. Clum

Sylvia E. Bowman, *Editor*

INDIANA UNIVERSITY

The career of Ridgely Torrence is one of the mysteries in the history of American poetry. When his first volume, *The House of a Hundred Lights*, appeared at the turn of the century, Torrence was hailed as a bright new talent. In 1905 the *Atlantic Monthly* devoted four pages to an article entitled "Mr. Torrence's Metrical Art" which sang the praises of his recently published "The Lesser Children." Twenty years later, when *Hesperides* appeared, critics praised it for containing ". . . some of the most definite and distinguished poetry of the day." By that time his poems "The Son," "Eye Witness," and "The Bird in the Tree" had become anthology pieces. His Negro plays comprised in the eyes of many critics a crucial episode in the history of the American theater. Robert Frost, a poet not known for offering tributes to his colleagues, subtitled his poem "A Passing Glimpse," "To Ridgely Torrence: On Last Looking Into His Hesperides." Despite this recognition and praise, Torrence is virtually forgotten two decades after his death. His volumes are out of print, and literary history has chosen to forget his contribution.

A fresh look at Ridgely Torrence's work shows that history has not been completely just to the Ohio-born poet. Torrence was a lyricist closely tied to the mid-western soil from which he sprang, and his best work has a simple, almost rustic flavor. His successful lyrics are characterized by simplicity, grace, and mastery of poetic technique, but his technical skill is not the only claim Ridgely Torrence has to our attention. His writings show a deep concern for his fellow man. The compassion shown for the black man about to be lynched in "The Bird in the Tree," the sensitivity to the suffering of America's first citizens in "The Feasters," and the overpowering sense of the horror

wn in such works as "Peace" and ן King Edge" demonstrate a ocial conscience. It must have e courage in 1917 to present a the black man's hatred of white lay, "Granny Maumee," was the an attempt at writing a serious Negroes. Throughout his career work always embodied an the best that is in man to iis hatred and cruelty.

first book-length study of the dgely Torrence. Because of this, e contains not only extensive of Torrence's work, published ished, but also a glimpse at the oet and the literary associations ced his work.

E AUTHOR

lum, a member of the English at Duke University, received his Ph.D. degrees from Princeton His fields of interest are literature, twentieth-century film, as well as the problems of cation, a subject on which he has a number of articles. He was Outstanding Professor at Duke in s presently Director of Duke's use for Academic and Residen- nentation.

RIDGELY TORRENCE

FREDERIC RIDGELY TORRENCE

lew York

TO MY PARENTS

Preface

THIS book is the first full-length study of the career of Frederick Ridgely Torrence—poet, playwright, editor, biographer, and critic; but it might be more accurate to describe this volume as a study of Torrence's careers, for each of these facets of his professional life was important to the history of American literature in the twentieth century. As is the case with so many "forgotten" but important figures in the history of American literature, there is nothing sensational about the career of Ridgely Torrence. The quantity of his literary output is not overwhelming; his work was respected and admired by the critics from the very beginning, but it never achieved popular success. During his years on the editorial staffs of *The Critic, Cosmopolitan,* and *The New Republic,* not only was he in a very influential position, but he used this position to be of great help to a number of aspiring American poets. He gained such affection and respect from his colleagues that he was elected one of the first chairmen of the Academy of American Poets. His close friends included such figures as Edwin Arlington Robinson, William Vaughn Moody, Edwin Markham, Robert Frost, and Edmund Clarence Stedman. Still, Torrence himself never attained the status of a major American poet.

A rereading of Torrence's canon, however, convinces one of his mastery of the tools of his trade. Some of the works that are discussed in this study warrant close scrutiny and are worthy of a high place in American poetry. The poetry contained in the *Hesperides* volume certainly deserves Louis Untermeyer's comment that its pages contain "some of the most definite and distinguished poetry of the day." But there is another reason for embarking upon a discussion of Torrence's work: his career mirrors some of the important trends in American poetry of this century. He began to write under the influence of the late Victorians and of the poets of America's Gilded Age who specialized in the exotic and the hedonistic. He was active in the movement toward an American poetic drama during the first decade of this century; and, when his colleagues turned to the writing of prose dramas, Torrence, too, tried his hand at this medium. About the time that Robert Frost published *A Boy's Will* (1913), Torrence began writing regional poems set in his native Greene County, Ohio. After J. M. Synge rose to prominence with his native Irish folk theater, Torrence attempted to create its American counterpart with his plays for Negroes. An inspection of Torrence's work allows us to explore, therefore, these many areas of interest to American poets.

Perhaps the aspect of Torrence's career for which he will be most remembered is his important contribution to the role of the Negro in American literature. Before Torrence's three Negro plays, there had been no *serious* drama about the Negro in America. Negroes were presented either as faithful, if stupid, servants, or as comic characters. Torrence presented the Negro not only as a viable dramatic character but also as a serious actor in the legitimate theater. From the first presentation of his Negro plays, Torrence was intimately associated with the place of the Negro in American life and letters. He studied the Negro theater in America for the Rockefeller Foundation, and he culminated his career with a superb biography of Negro educator John Hope.

This study concentrates upon Torrence's work, but to divorce an examination of his canon from an understanding of the social and literary forces at work on its creator is neither sensible nor possible. So much of Torrence's creative output was directly affected by his background and the literary figures with whom he associated that some biographical material is necessary. Moreover, a study of Torrence's life affords some new insights into the personalities of many of his associates. The biographical material used in this study is taken from the rich collection of Torrence materials housed in the Princeton University Library. This collection, filling one hundred and twenty-five boxes, provides not only the materials for a full study of Torrence but also many important documents relating to his colleagues. In preparing my discussion of the poems and plays, I have referred both to the volumes of collected poems and to the magazine versions. Unless otherwise noted, the version cited is that of Torrence's final version as contained in the volumes of collected poems. Since all of

Preface

Torrence's published output is now out of print, the discussions of his works are documented by a generous amount of quotation.

This volume is likely to stand for a while as the only book on Ridgely Torrence. This fact led me to include more biographical data than is the norm in this series. My hope is that the book not only offers the student an introduction to Torrence but also provides a trustworthy source for scholars of American literary history.

I wish to offer my thanks to my friend and former teacher, Willard Thorp, for his generosity and his encyclopedic knowledge. In addition, my thanks to Mrs. Jean Torrence Bales, Torrence's niece; to the staff of the Manuscript Division of the Princeton University Library, especially Mrs. Wanda Randall, for their able assistance; to Mrs. Hugh Bullock, Malcolm Cowley, Bruce Bliven, and Harriet Hegler of the Xenia City Schools for their useful information; and to Kathryne Brown, Richard Cytowic, and Michael Lyle for their work in preparing the manuscript.

JOHN M. CLUM

Duke University

Acknowledgments

Grateful acknowledgment is made to The Macmillan Company for permission to quote from the following volumes:

Poems by Ridgely Torrence. Copyright 1941 by The Macmillan Company.

Poems by Ridgely Torrence. Copyright 1952 by The Macmillan Company.

Three Plays for the Negro Theatre by Ridgely Torrence. Copyright 1917 by The Macmillan Company renewed 1945 by Ridgely Torrence.

Hesperides by Ridgely Torrence. Copyright 1925 by The Macmillan Company renewed 1953 by Olivia H. D. Torrence.

The Story of John Hope by Ridgely Torrence. Copyright 1948 by Ridgely Torrence.

Selected Letters of Edwin Arlington Robinson. Copyright 1940 by The Macmillan Company.

Edwin Arlington Robinson by Hermann Hagedorn. Copyright 1938 by Hermann Hagedorn renewed 1966 by Dorothy Hagedorn.

Also, grateful acknowledgment is due to Charles Scribner's Sons for permission to quote from Torrence's *Abelard and Heloise,* and to Holt, Rinehart and Winston, Inc., for permission to reprint from "A Passing Glimpse" from *Complete Poems of Robert Frost.* Copyright 1928 by Holt, Rinehart and Winston, Inc. Copyright 1956 by Robert Frost. And to Anna D. Partridge and Olive H. Barbour for permission to quote from those poems by Torrence to which they hold the rights.

Contents

Contents

Chronology

1874   Frederick Ridgely Torrence born November 22 in Xenia, Ohio.

1893   Enters Miami College, Ohio. Contributor to *The Miami Student*.

1895   Enters Princeton University as special student. Writer for *The Nassau Literary Magazine;* performs with the Triangle Club.

1896   December, asked to withdraw from Princeton for medical reasons. Moves to New York City.

1897   "Astarte" published in August issue of *New England Magazine.* Secures position at Astor Library.

1899   Meets Edmund Clarence Stedman. Publication of *The House of a Hundred Lights.*

1900   Inclusion in *An American Anthology.* Friendships with Edwin Arlington Robinson and Josephine Preston Peabody. Begins *El Dorado.*

1903   August, publication of *El Dorado;* September, begins work as assistant editor of *The Critic.*

1904   Publication of "The Masque of Hours" in March issue of *The Critic.* Summer spent in Xenia recuperating from paratyphoid.

1905   March, accepts post as fiction editor of *Cosmopolitan.* September, publication in *The Atlantic Monthly* of "The Lesser Children."

1907   February, publication of *Abelard and Heloise;* works on prose dramas. Alla Nazimova interested in producing play, "The Madstone." March, Torrence and William Vaughn Moody begin trip around Mediterranean.

1908   At work on short lyrics. "Three O'Clock" published in December in *Scribner's Magazine.*

1909   Creation of "Rituals." Publication of "Ritual for Birth and Naming" and "The Ritual for Marriage" in *Century Magazine.*

1910 October, death of William Vaughn Moody. Torrence becomes interested in Thomas Troward's Mental Science.

1913 "Santa Barbara Beach" in March issue of *Poetry: A Magazine of Verse.* First of a series of lyrics published during the next decade in *Poetry, Scribner's Magazine, The Nation, The New Republic.*

1915 "A Vision of Spring" first poem to be printed in *The New Republic* (March 20).

1917 April 5, opening of Torrence's Negro plays at Garden Theater. Production moved to Garrick Theater on April 16, but survived for only one week. Becomes involved in pacifist activities.

1919 Beginning of friendship with Robert Frost.

1920 Visiting Professor of English at Miami University for academic year 1920–21; becomes poetry editor of *The New Republic.*

1925 Publication of *Hesperides,* first major volume of collected poems. Enthusiastic critical reception.

1933 Resigns from *The New Republic.*

1934 Helps found the Academy of American Poets.

1935 April 6, death of E. A. Robinson. Torrence ends ten-year "dry period" and resumes writing.

1936 Publication of "Outline" in May 30 issue of *Saturday Review of Literature.* First of a number of new poems published during next decade in *Saturday Review, The New Republic* and *Poetry: A Magazine of Verse.*

1937 Elected chairman of Academy of American Poets.

1938 Visiting Professor at Antioch College.

1939 Prepares study of Negro theater in America under auspices of Rockefeller Foundation.

1940 Edits and writes introduction for *Selected Letters of Edwin Arlington Robinson* for Macmillan.

1941 *Poems by Ridgely Torrence.*

1942 Visiting Professor at Miami University.

1947 Recipient of $5,000 fellowship from Academy of American Poets.

1948 *The Story of John Hope,* written under auspices of a grant from the Carnegie Corporation.

1950 Dies of lung cancer on Christmas Day.

1952 Revised edition of *Poems by Ridgely Torrence.*

CHAPTER 1

The House of a Hundred Lights

That's the hill that bore me, there I
    watch the grasses
In my father's keep.
All they knew before me gently passes
In the winds of sleep.

There the sounds are slender, there
    the Dreamer growing
With the song he sings
Smiles to find the tender evening glow-
    ing
With a look of wings.[1]

THE story of Ridgely Torrence's literary career begins like a novel by Theodore Dreiser. One cold winter day, just before Christmas in 1896, a young man stepped off a train in Weehawken and took the ferry across the Hudson River to Manhattan to begin a career as a writer. The young man was from Xenia, Ohio, one of those bustling midwestern towns that are so much a part of American myth, tradition, and reality. He had just been asked to leave Princeton for rather personal reasons, reasons that suggest that the young man was already beginning to extend the mores of his staunch United Presbyterian background. As a matter of fact, the idea of a career as a writer was in itself a departure from the way of life that his father, a Civil War captain, a successful lumber dealer, and a pillar of the community, wished for his son.

Ridgely Torrence had much in his favor as he entered the big city: he had an excellent, if incomplete education; he was good looking; and he was blessed with a puckish charm that was very appealing. More importantly, he was ambitious and determined to make his mark in American literature. All these qualities remained an integral part of his character during a career that spanned the first half of the twentieth century. But, if we are to understand Torrence's work and the directions it took, we must retrace the incidents that antedated Torrence's arrival in New York.

I *Juvenilia*

Few American authors could claim stronger ties to the land of which they sang than Ridgely Torrence. His ancestry certainly exemplified two of the major concerns of his poetry: freedom of the human spirit and man's relationship to the divine force. John Torrence, Ridgely's great-grandfather, helped plan the town of Lexington, Kentucky, in 1789; for he had been given a large grant of land as a reward for his service in the Revolutionary War. John Torrence himself had a noteworthy background. His mother was the youngest sister of Dr. Samuel Finley, fifth president of the College of New Jersey (now Princeton University) from 1761 to 1769. Another of Finley's nephews, Dr. Benjamin Rush, was a signer of the Declaration of Independence.

In 1804, John Torrence sold his holdings in Lexington and moved north to Xenia in the territory of Ohio which in that year became one of the United States. From then on, Xenia was the home of the Torrence family. Thus Ridgely's ancestors were, in a strong sense, pioneers who helped build the new territories in what was then the western frontier. Like many of the pioneers, the Torrences were first motivated to come to the New World by religious persecution in Great Britain. The Torrences were members of a body who called themselves "Seceders." They were Scottish Covenanters who had been driven out of Scotland into northern Ireland by seventeenth-century religious persecutions. Thus, the religious spirit of their descendants was as strong as their pioneer spirit. Their austere religion would not even recognize Christmas because they believed it to be a pagan festival.

While Torrence's father was descended from the early settlers of Xenia, his mother had come there from Maryland as an orphan at the age of twelve to stay with relatives. Mary Ridgely's marriage to Findley David Torrence, lumber dealer and former captain in the Civil War, was a happy one. Their temperaments complemented one another, for, as Torrence wrote of them, "He shared with my mother an ecstatic appreciation of the pageant of life but whereas her nature was eternally resilient and rebounded quickly from all the blows of fortune, he had a vein of melancholia, probably derived from his dour and austere Gaelic forbears." [2]

Their first child, Frederick Ridgely Torrence, was born on November 27, 1874. The circumstances of his birth were attended by the ill fortune that seemed to follow him through much of his life. Moreover, they suggest the strength of the superstitions of the Negroes who lived around Xenia—the supersitions that later provided the inspiration for his *Granny Maumee*. The mulatto woman who had long been a servant of the Torrence family was also skilled as a midwife; and, long before her time for delivery, Mrs. Torrence had arranged that this woman would help bring her child into the world. Two days before Ridgely's birth, when Mrs. Torrence asked the woman to be on hand the next day, the woman told Mrs. Torrence that she would try to be there but that she was sure her husband was going to kill her that night. The woman's prediction came true, and Mrs. Torrence was left to find someone else to help with the delivery. Unfortunately, she chose a young doctor who was a morphine addict, and he spent most of her period of labor in a stupor.

If the circumstances of Ridgely Torrence's birth were far from poetic, the time of his birth seemed right for the nurture of an American poet. At the beginning of an unpublished memoir, Torrence places himself in the context that will be most important to him and sets the scene for his development as a literary artist:

In the year in which I recall my first emotions and cerebral consciousness, 1877, Emerson was seventy-four, Alcott was seventy-eight, Whitman was fifty-eight, and Thoreau was fifteen years dead. Mark Twain at forty-two had just published *Tom Sawyer* and was collaborating with Bret Harte in a play which opened in Washington in 1877. In England, Browning was sixty-five, Stevenson at twenty-seven was contributing to the Cornhill and other magazines, Swinburne at forty was at the peak of his literary activity . . . and Hardy at thirty-seven was on the point of publishing *The Return of the Native*.

And in Gardiner, Maine, a fat sensitive, but excitedly happy boy with a blazingly flushed face crowned with black curls was breathlessly reading rhymes in the Robinson household, while in New Albany, Indiana, across the Ohio from Louisville, in Steam-

boat Captain Moody's house another seven year old boy with a
face like a faun, turned up nose, oblique eyes and golden curls,
was engaged feverishly in the same exciting and life surrendering
devotion.[3]

The story of Ridgely Torrence's early years is, in a sense, the
story of an exile. Although he did not divorce himself from his
country as the expatriates of the 1920's did, we cannot help feeling
that Torrence's separation from his Ohio country and his never-
ending sense of conflict with its values was a crucial element
in his personal and artistic life. At the core of his being, even
as an aspiring New York socialite, was Xenia, its traditions and its
values. It was only when Torrence began drawing on his home-
land as the basis of his work that he reached the peak of his powers. Despite the fact that his life from 1897 was centered in New
York City, the loss of the nomination for Ohio Poet Laureate in
1936 was a great disappointment to him. He always felt very close
to the Ohio soil: "Ohio inspired in me, in my childhood and boyhood, a strong attachment that seems only to increase as I grow
older. And the periods that I have spent there during my adult life
have been times of deep contentment. I ask no greater satisfaction
than to tramp over Ohio fields, in the early autumn, hunting
mushrooms, or to have a long unhurried talk with some neighbor
or childhood friend who always lived close to that rich soil and
who speaks the familiar friendly idiom." [4] It is interesting to note
that this 1936 statement was written in Torrence's study in New
York City. There was still a dimension lacking in what Xenia had
to offer Torrence, both as man and as artist.

Two of Torrence's boyhood years were spent, not in Xenia,
but in Santa Ana, California, and there is little doubt that the
memories of this exotic locale led to Torrence's later interest in
writing a play about the Spanish explorers. In fact, Torrence's
sense of his American heritage could not help being strengthened
by the frontier spirit of California in the 1880's. As he later wrote:
"What I don't forget are the sights, smells, touches and general
impact of California on my senses in those golden first hours fifty
years ago. The air, the setting was like paradise to me." [5]

Despite these vivid memories of Santa Ana, it was Xenia that
exerted the strongest influence. A description of this growing mid-
western town is similar to that of many American towns of this

period. Xenia was a village of eight thousand people, most of whose breadwinners were merchants of some sort or another or were connected with the town's major industry, the manufacture of twine and cordage. While up-to-date in architecture, communications, and transportation, it was spoiled, in a sense, by its very modernity. A steam railroad ran right along the main street of the city. The earlier frame dwellings and simple stores had been replaced by the inevitable square brick business area in which all the stores looked the same. In spite of these wounds of progress, Xenia's closest ties were still to the past. The town lies in the heart of Greene County, fifteen miles southeast of Dayton; and, despite the semi-industrial character of Xenia, Greene County remained a rural area of rolling slopes, brooks, and small farms inhabited by families much like those that had settled the area early in the century. Religion was central to the lives of the people of Xenia, and the dozen-odd churches were the most important buildings in town. The Torrences were devout United Presbyterians, and they subscribed to all the tenets of the "Protestant Ethic." Success in this world was measured by material security and by a sense of personal righteousness. Without consciously intending to, Ridgely would come into conflict with these values many times in the early years of his career.

Ridgely's education began in January, 1881, when he entered the first grade at the North School. It was not long before he developed a great love for reading, especially poetry:

It is hard to recall the first impact of rhyme or metre on my consciousness—that is, verbal rhythm. Year after year in my school life I was supplied with the successive anthologies of prose and verse, known as Readers—First, Second, Third, etc. On the first day of each year's school term, I voraciously devoured the contents of the year's volume. That book contained exclusively the final sum and ultimate extent of every and any conceivable interest to me in the school curriculum. From that first day, the year to me was void of any possibility, so far as I remember, of arresting my scholastic attention. Day after day, throughout the hours of imprisonment while other subjects were being imposed upon the class, I could surreptitiously hold my Reader under my desk and furtively con the well remembered and already boring measures of Bryant's lines to a Waterfowl, Longfellow's Wreck of the Hesperus, Holmes' The Last Leaf or the Chambered Nautilus.[6]

Ridgely's record at the North School was good except for arithmetic, which seems to have suffered from the young scholar's lack of interest in nonliterary subjects. He left the North School after the sixth grade when he and his family moved to California. When he returned to Xenia, he resumed his studies at a small private school run by Miss Anna McCracken.

In the fall of 1893, Ridgely enrolled at Miami University, then a small college whose students came mostly from the surrounding Ohio counties. The primitive living conditions at Miami inspired Ridgely to write his mother: "It is a good thing I took a good bath while at home, it is very cold and there are so little facilities for bathing that I am sorry to say I have not bathed since returning, so I will bring this letter to a close and try to hoe myself, or I will find myself returning to the aboriginal flint-hurling, anthropophagal anthropoid; clothed in a garment evolved from fig-leaves." [7] By his sophomore year he felt that the living conditions were not the only aspect of Miami that left something to be desired: "This year is quieter than last, there is absolutely nothing to break the monotony of the dull routine of the classroom. There has not been a single entertainment at the college. All this though is certainly conducive to study. A man would study under such circumstances and environments, simply for lack of something else to do, even if he had no other object." [8]

It is clear that these feelings of boredom did not stop Ridgely from working hard at Miami and, from the beginning, demonstrating his creative bent:

> I am to have honorable mention in English literature, as being the best in that department. That means to have your name printed on the programs Commencement Day. I am doing extra work, outside, continually for Dr. Hepburn, the Prof. in charge. I am in my element in it and like it ever so much, when I have completed my required work, which is at the end of the Soph. year, you know, I intend to take all of my work in that department. It will be a fine thing to be under Dean Murray who is head of the department at Princeton. [9]

This letter contains the first mention in Torrence's correspondence of his decision to transfer to Princeton. The move was probably inspired by Professor Roger Bruce Cash Johnson, who had been brought to Miami from Princeton some years before. John-

son's career was an impressive one: reared in the Bahamas, he had
gone as an undergraduate to Princeton where he had distinguished himself in languages and philosophy to such a degree that
he had had the honor of delivering the Latin Salutatory address at
his commencement and had earned the Fellowship in Mental Science that supported him for a year of graduate study. In 1888,
Johnson was appointed Professor of Mental and Moral Philosophy
at Miami University, a post he held for seventeen years. In
September, 1905, he returned to Princeton as one of Woodrow
Wilson's original group of preceptors. In 1910 he was made a
professor of philosophy and in 1926 became chairman of the
department, a post he held until his retirement in 1934.

As a philosopher, Johnson was much influenced by William
James and the British school of Neo-Hegelian idealists; and in his
teaching and writing he emphasized the relevance of psychology
to many of the central problems of philosophy. All records indicate that Johnson was an exciting and inspiring teacher, and there
seems to be little doubt that Torrence felt a measure of hero worship for this dynamic, ultrasophisticated philosopher: "I feel I
cannot overestimate the good that my association with him has
done. I value it as equal to, if not superior to, the training I have
gotten in the class room. He gave me ideas about men and things
and education when I first came to school last year, far different
from those which I previously had had. He has practically shown
me a world that I never would have known had it not been for
him." [10]

Johnson was probably instrumental not only in Torrence's personal development but also in his new-found interest in writing
poetry. Torrence's early attempts, published in *The Miami Student*, are colored with the hedonistic quality of the output of late
Victorian poets such as Swinburne, Rossetti, and Wilde. A characteristic example is the sonnet, "A Japanese Girl," which was published in *The Miami Student* in May, 1897, although it was written earlier:

A Japanese Girl

White, soft cream white and delicately slim,
    Like some fair gem carved from warm ivory,
    With deep eyes that rove downward slantingly,
To see her image in the teacup's brim

And seeing, blushes to the very rim
    And of burnished hair arranged fantastically.
  Then looking up with pretty tyranny,
She faintly frowns and tho' her frown is dim
  It makes us forget loves that we have known,
Forget all else but the desire to paint
Her portrait thus ere sweet shy youth has flown,
Leaving her bronzed and eerie-faced and quaint,
    To drone forth changings, when with golden moan,
  The temple gongs at eve sound far and faint.[11]

The *chinoiserie,* the emphasis on color, the idea of the desire to
re-create natural beauty through art—all these are characteristics
of much of "contemporary" poetry, especially that published in
the successful "literary" magazines. We might wonder at the fascination this type of poetry had for a small-town Ohio lad whose
background seemed to be firmly rooted in the American tradition.
There is no impulse to write from his own experience—of the region or of the people he knew, as Edwin Arlington Robinson did
—nor is there any of the metaphysical speculation that marked
William Vaughn Moody's early poetry. Torrence's inspiration
came from poetry rather than from life, and this separation of art
and life is certainly not surprising in the Gilded Age. Moreover,
we cannot help but notice in this early effort Torrence's fascination with form. Not only are the ground rules of the sonnet form
being followed here, but Torrence seems to delight in working
within such a rigid structure. This interest in the structural aspects
of a poem would be characteristic of all Torrence's work. Each
poem seems "experimental" in a sense, but the experiment always
involves a rigid structure.

There seems little doubt that Torrence's writing had become his
vocation. Not only did he devote much time to his creative en-
deavors during the school year, but he also used to hammer away
at his verse on the typewriter of his father's office during the summer months. His father used to gather the material Torrence
wrote there and save it, not out of pride in his son's work, but
because he suspected that the boy was losing his mind: "This
package contains verses written by Fred here in the office. When
on vacation from Miami University he would sit down at the
typewriter and hammer them off and go away and forget all
about them. I recognized the fact that something was the *matter*

with him. So I gathered them up from time to time, to hold as
evidence, in the event they should be needed." [12] Such an attitude
fortunately did not discourage this prodigal son, though Torrence
was quite aware of his father's disapproval of his poetic activity.

As planned, the poet-to-be enrolled in Princeton as a non-degree
student in the fall of 1895. His recollections of that moment could
be mistaken for those of Fitzgerald's Princetonian hero, Amory
Blaine:

> My first impressions of Princeton were certainly most favorable,
> the place is beautiful and far beyond my expectations. The cam-
> pus seems fully as large as the Miami campus and fully as beau-
> tiful as regards natural scenery and then added to this fact the
> place is made grander still by having about fifty magnificent
> stone buildings on it. Another thing that impressed me was the
> beauty of the town itself. Quite a good many very wealthy people
> live here and there are some magnificent buildings and splendid
> dwellings. I have heard Dr. Patton [President of the College]
> several times and listened to a very fine sermon which he preached
> Sabbath. The most beautiful building on campus is Alexander
> Hall, built of white and brown stone for an auditorium. . . .[13]

During his first term at Princeton, Ridgely took a rigorous
program of seven courses: physics, psychology, history of philosophy, art, astronomy, and Old English. His life was not confined to
the library, however; he made quite a name for himself in the
productions of the Princeton Triangle Club, that famous musical-
comedy organization that produced such notables as Booth Tarkington and Scott Fitzgerald. In the 1896 production, *The Mummy:
A High Old Egyptian Extravaganza*, young Ridgely graced
the boards as "Atessa, the maiden sister of the Rameses, with a
longing for love and corkscrew curls." [14] His new-found interest in
the stage did not, however, divert him from poetry; for he found
time to write poems for *The Nassau Literary Magazine*. Two
poems from the issues of January and February, 1896 demonstrate the same characteristics evident in "A Japanese Girl":

Silenus[15]

Ah! yestere'en, deep in a leafy nook
  I saw the sot, with senses held in thrall,
  His wreathed pate awry. I heard him call

Some wanton's name, babbling like any brook.
Besmeared with lees of wine, he caught and shook
  His pipes, all drooping, broken in some brawl.
  He stumbled, swayed, and, fearful lest he fall,
I hailed him, and he heard, and lo! his look
Grew sly and cautious, until by the dead
And rustling leaves my hiding place he learned.
  His satyr's face grew dim and faintly lined—
What seemed his body was the river's bed—
  The blossomed locks to water lilies turned—
  The broken pipes were reeds swept by the wind.

Receipt for a Song[16]

Oh! Always start with "Oh!" or "Ah!" might do.
Then choose the season and the time of day
Or night; and, having chosen, start your lay.
If spring, use "green," of course, and "winds that blew,"
A "thrush," a "lark" and "moist with falling dew."
But should you pipe "all on a Summer's day,"
Have "hot sun," "limpid rills" and "new-mown hay."
Give "Autumn leaves" a "sere and yellow" hue.
In Winter use the "crisp and frosty glare"
If your muse be Swinburne's—but if Browning's
Sing from chaotic, formless nothingness
Of preexistence, when you stood on air
Shudd'ring at dead faces and their frownings.
Use this, and you'll compose—well, who can guess?

Both poems are cast in the Italian sonnet form with the octave comprised of two *abba* quatrains and the sestet comprised of two triplets with the same rhyme scheme. However, Torrence does not use this structure to underscore the thematic movement of his sonnet. The octave and sestet are linked by the fact that there is no sentence break at the end of the eighth line as well as by the fact that there is no use of the rhetorical dimension of the sonnet structure. What is most interesting about these two poems, however, is the way in which they presage the two styles which Torrence later utilizes in *The House of a Hundred Lights*.

While both poems are in the same form, "Silenus" utilizes Classical myth and formal, poetic diction; but "Receipt for a Song" is informal and humorous. Both poems show that Torrence had learned well the method and language of the poets of his time;

however, "Silenus" and "Receipt for a Song" show a great deal of promise, and they obviously impressed the staff of the "Lit," for Torrence was elected to its editorial board in April, 1896. The appointment did much to bolster his confidence in his literary abilities, and he was quite conscious of the honor it represented: "It is considered by the faculty to be the highest literary honor in the college to be on the board of editors and it raises one very far in their estimation." [17]

It is clear from the letters written during his first year at Princeton that Ridgely was enthusiastic about all aspects of his life there. He certainly loved the extracurricular activities, and this aspect of his Princeton life led to an academic record that was far from distinguished. His letters home are characteristic of the promises of the student whose mind is not primarily on his work: "If there is anything in me, it is going to show this time, if by doing so I can lessen the burden of anxiety you bear for me." [18]

The last months of 1896 were to mark the end of Ridgely's college career. A disease contracted during the summer vacation prevented him from returning to Princeton until December, and his stay then was short. The exact nature of Torrence's illness is never mentioned in his letters; but, soon after he returned to Princeton, some of his classmates, fearing that he had a venereal disease that might be communicated through common use of the college lavatories, requested that the administration ask for his withdrawal. Torrence, who could not disprove the accusations of his peers, chose to withdraw voluntarily from the university and to find a job in New York City.

His letter to his father telling of his withdrawal vividly expresses the guilt the young man felt and his determination to prove himself by embarking upon a new career in the frightening metropolis: "Father, please try to bear up under this further overwhelming burden. I am not discouraged. I do not dare to be. If I allowed myself to be it would be death and I cannot die without doing something to redeem myself. I have decided that I must not return home without having put forth every effort and *I am determined* that I will get something to do." [19] The young man that left the Romanesque arches of Princeton for New York City was, therefore, a young man intent upon reinstating himself in his parents' eyes. Certainly the behavior that had led to his withdrawal from Princeton was antithetical to the standards of his

Calvinistic parents, and Ridgely could not help feeling that his parents could never trust him again; "I know I can't help myself or restrain my reckless nature, but I want you to know that I pray continually that I may be strengthened to do it, and so with God on my side I think you ought to feel more at ease, if indeed it is about me that you are troubled." [20]

But, if Ridgely had vestiges of the strong sense of guilt that was part of his heritage, he also had a great deal of the Torrence ambition. A plucky young man, he was resolved not to be defeated or discouraged. He moved into a mission house on Union Square and immediately began looking for a job. Astute enough to realize that the job had to be one in which he could support himself as well as involve his interest in writing, the obvious field for him was journalism; but it was not easy to break into the newspaper world, and Torrence had to make what money he could by peddling free-lance material to the New York *World*. Unfortunately, he was discovering that this writing did not provide enough money to live on; and he more than once had the frustrating experience of seeing his work under the by-line of some staff writer. Such experiences led him to modify his ambitions to some extent, but not in the direction of practicality:

> In the first place you ask if I have given up journalism. No, I have not by any means. I am more and more impressed all the time with the fact that I can do better in *certain branches* of it than in any other profession. Unfortunately for me these *certain branches* are the higher paths of literary achievement rather than the cheap, circulation building Sunday-news journalism of today which requires brawn in lieu of brains. And these "higher paths," altho' quite as lucrative if not more so, are only open to the elect, or in other words, to those who have made a name and reputation. And the only way to get that name and reputation is by the persistent grind that is necessary in all walks of life. So I keep turning out stories and like effusions and sending them in and getting them returned, but I have talent in that direction and I will make them notice me. [21]

These stories were typed out on a typewriter borrowed from a seminary student whom Ridgely knew at the mission. As could be expected, Torrence's literary ideas were in keeping with the current literary fashion:

You ask about the character of the writing I am doing. I have decided to cut out the verse part of it so that it will simply be a collection of stories. As to its moral effect, about which you ask, I think that if they are read at all (and that is the first consideration) their effect would be good rather than bad although they are not written to point a moral or to prove anything. They are written in a new style called Realism which depicts life as it is rather than what it ought to be and to that end it ought to be good, for instance: in one of the stories, a young man steals, the story then goes on to relate the further history of the man and in it is seen how in the natural course of events, retribution is visited upon him. The story does not attempt to demonstrate the punishment of thievery but merely says that under certain conditions at such and such a time, certain things happened and you may take them for what you may or draw what moral for yourself but above all this is the Truth and not fiction or a work of art to please.[22]

It is obvious that Torrence had been reading the work of the leading exponents of the Realistic school. None of these early stories are extant, but we doubt if Torrence's previous experience equipped him to be a short-story writer in the Realistic vein. Certainly the editors were not impressed, and Torrence found himself still in need of a job that would make him financially independent of his overburdened parents. Finally, in June, 1896, six months after he had moved to New York, Torrence secured a position on the staff of the New York Public Library. The work was arduous, especially in the heat of summer, the hours were long, and the pay was meager. Still, it was better than nothing; for it offered a measure of financial security. As for Torrence's long-range plans at this time, he wrote his parents to say: "I have almost given up all hope of going back to college. I have but two ambitions, the first to help you, and the second, to make a name in American literature." [23]

Ridgely's zeal toward his literary work was unflagging, and in the summer of 1897 good news came. His poem "Astarte" was accepted for publication in the August issue of *New England Magazine*. "Astarte" was inspired by the mural John Singer Sargent had recently created for the Boston Public Library. Sargent's inspiration was the passage on Istaroth, one of the pagan goddesses, in John Milton's *Paradise Lost*. Torrence provided his explanation of the character and his conception of his poem in a letter to his parents: "Istar or Astarte or Ashtaroth was the old

Assyrian moon goddess, corresponding to the Venus of Grecian mythology. She was the Assyrian conception of the embodiment of fleshly desire or the lust of the flesh. . . . I wrote the piece in defiance of the vice of which she is the symbol and showed (symbolically) that I was, far from being caught in her snares, her master because I could turn her very terrors to the uses of my art and make them a thing of beauty." [24]

The poem itself embodies some interesting aspects of Torrence's poetry at the time. Its topic is sexual desire, but Torrence was still too much of a product of his background to see this as anything but evil. Torrence sees Astarte as a Circe-like character luring men to their ruin, but there is no sense of allurement. Rather, the poem is filled with images of violence and pain. Once again, Torrence has chosen the Italian sonnet form, and "Astarte" demonstrates the same facility with elevated poetic diction that we find in his student work:

Astarte
(after seeing Sargent's fresco in the Boston Library) [25]

Deep in my heart's dim halls still lies enshrined
That awe-full sight; the calm, unhuman face;
That pois'nous curved mouth I still can trace;
While all around, about her and behind,
Circled her soulless maids, and I defined
Their beckoning white arms across the space.
Her pale blue web of death like wondrous lace
Floated, and yet was driven by no wind;
For, Ah! those waving folds were tossed and thrown
With writhings of mashed souls that writhe in vain
To free themselves; nor shriek'd nor made they moan,
But silent waved, like drowned limbs seen through rain;—
And through the veil, among the souls, mine own
Looked back at me, its face grown gray with pain.

Torrence clearly has internalized the contemporary style to the point at which he is comfortable with it, for there is no sign here of strain. As a result, "Astarte" is a well-made poem. Yet it is remote from human experience, and here we see the most basic problem for a poet of the 1890's.

At a time in which art is seen by the poetic establishment as being separated from life and as operating in a realm of the

"Ideal," a poet's only impetus is art itself and his poetry must inevitably suffer from eclecticism. Emily Dickinson escaped this trap by isolating herself from the pressures that would operate on an artist; and Stephen Crane, perhaps the most revolutionary poet of the period, did not like to see his poetry recognized by "the establishment." American poets still looked to Europe for their models because the new American plutocracy that set the styles and supported the artists equated Culture with the Old World. Torrence had not yet met Edmund Clarence Stedman, the unofficial poet laureate of the age; but Stedman's esthetic pervades Torrence's early work, as we can see from this excerpt from Stedman's "The Hillside Door":

> For where yon pillars are,
> And birds with tuneful voices call,
> There shines a star,—
> The crown she wears, the Fairy Queen of all!
> Led to that inmost wooded haunt
> By maidens ministrant,
> I halt afar.
>
> O joy! she sees me stand
> Doubting, and calls me near her throne,
> And waves her wand,
> As in my dreams, and smiles on me alone.
> O royal beauty, proud and sweet!
> I bow me at her feet
> To kiss that hand:
>
> Ah woe! ah, fate malign!
> By what a rude revengeful gust,
> From that fair shrine
> Which holds my sovran mistress I am thrust!
> Then comes a mocking voice's taunt,
> Crying, *Thou fool, avaunt!*
> *She is not thine!* [26]

This sort of rococo word painting was what much of American poetry had descended to in the 1890's, and Torrence was only too able as an imitator. Fortunately, this topic of the soul's conflict with some sort of personification of sensual desire did not interest the young aspirant for long.

Torrence's next experiments were with what he hoped would be a distinctly American poetic utterance: "the first rule I have chosen in trying to make my verses typically American is to speak (or sing) (Figuratively) at the top of my voice, for above all things Americans are loud and self assertive among nations." [27] Torrence, in Whitmanesque fashion, set out to write a volume of American poetry entitled "Poems: Dedicated to the spirit of song in America, which is, and was, and shall be." [28] The title was suitably general, if a bit bombastic, as the poems are varied in type and intent. Unfortunately, Torrence's style in these works reflects much more of Stedman than of Whitman. This influence is best seen in the sonnet dedicated to Whitman, one of the six poems on American poets in this projected volume:

> O strident-voiced, clear-eyed, fibrous, fierce, tanned,
> Man-intoxicated spirit, what new word
> Is there to sing to men, they have not heard
> Already from you, yet stretch forth your hand
> And lend the lesser singers of the land
> Your aid to live nor let them be deterr'd
> By the thin shadows. Laud or Blame, but gird
> Them with your thews, teach them to stand.
> Teach them to stand as you stood among men
> Stood and sung and lived nor bent the knee
> To any image or any denizen
> Of earth or heaven or underneath the sea
> Like one of Israel's prophets, born again
> That saw God face to face, for each was He. [29]

There is an irony in this poem that certainly eluded Torrence, for this tribute represents just the sort of irrelevant, archaic poetry against which Whitman rebelled. Instead of reflecting the energy of Whitman, the sonnet only demonstrates the atrophy of the so-called Genteel Tradition. It is interesting to note, too, that the sonnet form is irrelevant. The poem may have fourteen lines, most of which are iambic pentameter, but the choice of form seems an arbitrary one. Interesting, too, is the fact that Torrence seems to be straining against the iambic pentameter line here. There are many lines in which he drops the convention in favor of a freer, varied rhythm. Perhaps Whitman's spirit was, after all, exerting a salutary effect on the young poet.

The variety of forms used by Torrence in the projected volume demonstrates an interest in experimenting with different forms. One of the most interesting works in the collection is "Bacchics," a purely hedonistic poem that is, in a loose sense, Classical in form but without the ethical dimension that characterized the "Classical" poetry of Tennyson and Arnold. We are also reminded of the Choric songs in Moody's *The Fire Bringer,* but there they are in the context of a larger and richer work. In "Bacchics" Torrence seems to relish the challenge of writing within this restrictive form. The content is totally subservient to form; but, at this stage in Torrence's career, and at this juncture in the history of American poetry, such is to be expected:

Bacchics[30]
———

Vine
And heart of the vine
Grow
Twine
In the shade and the shrine;
Blow
Your tinted bubbles for my love and me
Riper than her lips they cannot be
Nor ever so.

———

Shade
Green leaves making shade
Cool,
Layed
On the brow of the maid,
Rule
My youth's hot blood 'tho even you do share
Your coolness with the shadow of her hair
And her eyes' pool.

———

Dance
Swift whirl of the dance
Turn.

Enhance
Her too calm glance
Burn
Her sweet, cool blood as mine is burning now
She knows not yet Love's sweet and treads too slow
The way to learn.

———

Song
Love's maddn'ning song,
Silence.
Long
I've left the gay throng
Thence
I fled to you for no song seemed so sweet
My girl, as your mere breath, its gentle heat
Is recompence.

The most interesting poem in the collection was the "Ballad of
the Lost Soul," an eleven-stanza poem surprisingly spare in image
and metaphor but much richer in content than the works that
preceded it. In it, Torrence uses an extremely simple story which
belies a crucial and serious theme—the nature of man's relation to
God. The language, too, is very simple, similar to that used in his
later regional poems such as "The Son":

Ballad of the Lost Soul [31]

On a stirless, starless night
Dark through the sky's cup
A soul was loosed from out our sight,
From where men mourn and sup,
And floated up

Up through the past the air we breathe
An infinite long way.
It saw the night it left behind
But it was where the suns obey
Eternal day.

And now the soul was with all those
Of that expectant throng

That wait and sing to God, who knows
What is in each one's song
Of good or wrong.

For their souls sing what their lives sang
When they were living here,
There were some rang true but many rang
False and fell harsh and drear
Upon God's ear.

They saw, the soul must have been one
Of earth's rich who are poor
For he was shamed by that sun
That always shines before
God's golden door.

Within the porches of God's place
No priest nor prophet stood
But a slim form with a child's face
Made all the place seem good
As lilies would.

His feet just touched the upper tips
Of what were clouds I guess
His eyes were lifted and his lips
Forever curved in a caress
Of lovingness.

The soul looked long about the place
Then asked the child and said;
"Where is the lord? I seek his face,
Yet only find you here instead
You and these dead."

O then the white one bent his head
Out from the porches rim
And to the soul he answered
"God only knows those who know him."
His eyes were dim.

His eyes were dim for the large tears
We saw ere they were gone.
But they *fell on unheeding ears*,
For, seeing in the east, the dawn
The soul sped on.

And as the White One watch'd it go
Slow to the brink he trod
And look'd until it sank below,
Then blessed those waiting, with a nod,
For he was God.

This poem is the beginning of the simple, direct style of folk poetry that characterizes Torrence's best mature work. The poem is eclectic and is obviously influenced by some of the sentimental, quasi-religious magazine poetry of the time and by the vagabond poetry of Bliss Carman and Richard Hovey; but Torrence's contribution is a simplicity and economy that became his hallmark. Moreover, the poem is the first of Torrence's works to demonstrate the strain of mysticism that dominates his later lyrics.

No publisher showed interest in a volume from the pen of an unknown poet at a time when the public's first interest was the Spanish-American War, and the material in Torrence's first collection has been relegated to the category of unpublished juvenilia. Torrence remained undaunted, however. If the reading public did not want poetry at this time, he would write political tracts. He wrote a monograph entitled "The Soul of Man Under Socialism" and became interested in defending Socialist views in his work: "I have become a thorough going socialist as is every thinking man at heart nowadays. Perfect satisfaction with existing conditions is only the state of mind of an inanimate object. . . . I see plainly that the singer of the future has got to come down from the palace of art and sing to men and of men and be one of them." [32]

Unfortunately, Torrence did not continue to practice what he preached. One major reason for his not joining his contemporaries, Crane and Robinson, at this time by writing verse that verbalized his new-found social concern and metaphysical doubts was the strong ties he still felt to his parents and the world of Xenia. Torrence's father wrote him that poems on "Souls and Socialism and other abominable rot . . . teaches nothing but crank ideas." [33] This comment is indicative of the attitude the young writer's parents had toward his literary ambition. Their hope was that he would become settled in some practical, lucrative profession, and lead the God-fearing life espoused by the good people of Xenia. Because of this conflict in values, and Torrence's inability to break his ties of dependence on his family, he repeatedly felt the need to justify himself to his parents:

No one realizes better than I just how much my kind of writing amounts to but the trouble is that it is the only kind that I am capable of doing. I know my self sufficient talk about genius made you skeptical and tired but I merely wanted you to feel that I was interested in something (a thing which you always discredited). Now I know that it will not be any great power to lift men up and I am not sure but you have hit the nail when you say "imbibed & not inspired," but my hope is that it will lead up to some work that will help men and where I can find my natural element. No great work was ever written by a boy of my age but at my age they have proved that they had something in them to hope for and that is what I hope for myself. I do not regret not having been a financier, it would be as wrong as it would be in vain. The only thing to do is to make the best of what is given me. I have dropped that "shroud and grave" verse writing and am constantly reaching out and trying to see what I *can* do best. It was in this striving that I have been studying sociology and wrote a treatise.[34]

This statement certainly demonstrates that Torrence's thinking about his poetry was moving in the right direction for a poet of his time; but the necessity for making this sort of justification to the people who meant most to him could not help but be frustrating to the lonely young man, struggling to begin a career in a profession in which the chances for success were slim. As loving and devoted as he was toward his family, it was clear that he needed someone who would understand his interests and ambitions rather than criticize them, who would understand his doubts about some of the dogmas with which he grew up. This type of moral support would not come from Xenia. He needed another adviser like Professor Johnson at Miami. During the next twelve months, Torrence would not only gain such a friend but also a publisher.

II *Stedman and Bidpai*

The year 1899 proved to be a crucial one in Torrence's career. The eager, but somewhat frustrated poet-to-be finally was beginning to see some signs of recognition. The reason for this encouragement was a project quite different from any that he had previously attempted. Inspired by Edward FitzGerald's translation of *The Rubaiyat of Omar Khayyam*, Torrence became interested in Persian poetry. Gottheil, the Jewish Rabbi who had charge of the

Oriental collection at the Astor Library, taught him some basic
Persian and suggested that he read the work of Bidpai, an Indian
sage of the third century A.D., who was translated into Persian in
the sixth and eighth centuries. A number of the fables of Bidpai
had been translated into English by Sir Thomas North, but Torrence does not mention having read an English translation. In
fact, Torrence's letters suggest that he was unaware that the Persian translation with which he became familiar was not the original.

Bidpai's fables, considered by some scholars to be the first examples of beast fables, were originally written for the edification
of an Indian prince. The fables themselves are designed to be
exempla of princely behavior and are interspersed with couplets
containing bits of behavioral advice. It was these couplets that
interested Torrence. His opinion of Bidpai is interesting, for he
saw him in very "American" terms: "This solitary observer of
men's ways in a far off century and country found, just as he
would find now among us, much to weep for, even more to laugh
at notwithstanding that he does laugh more than he weeps. He is
the intellectual ancestor of Abraham Lincoln, a monument of
plain horse sense very beautifully spoken." [35] Not only did Torrence involve himself in his translation of the Bidpai couplets; he
was also inspired to devote a sonnet to his task:

On Translating Bidpai[36]

Into this world of visible images
This fleshly body drew my shrinking soul
Seized it, and heeded not its shrieks, but stole
Thro' Gates of Birth into unloveliness
And Oh, the smoky way and fret and stress
And striving of Art's face against Gain's goal
And songs wine mock'd with many an empty bowl
Bred in my heart such quiv'ring emptyness
That I was feign to flee, but then came one
And with a father's voice spoke low and long
And bade me know the day was not yet done
And ask'd "What were the Good without the Wrong?"
For he himself had suffered, sung and won
This giant of the elder world of song.

It is not in the least surprising that the young poet should become fascinated with such a project. Since its first anonymous

publication in 1859, *The Rubaiyat of Omar Khayyam* had achieved a phenomenal success both in England and in America. For any young poet who aspired to material as well as artistic success, the success that Edward FitzGerald had had with his re-working of the Persian's quatrains would certainly have provided some sort of inspiration. The little-known Bidpai would seem a likely candidate for the duplication of this success. Like FitzGer-ald, Torrence was not so much interested in a literal translation as he was in an adaptation of the couplets to suit the taste of the time. Many of the verses he produced were, therefore, more Tor-rence than Bidpai.

The first draft of the Bidpai adaptations were sent to Small, Maynard and Company of Boston in November, 1898. Three months later Maynard wrote Torrence that, "in their present shape," he did not deem them fit for publication, but he thought that they could be revised so as to be in acceptable shape. The principal source of Maynard's objections was the uneven quality of the poetry, but he felt that revision could bring the entire work to the level of its best parts. Torrence, encouraged by the letter, was sure that he could revise the work so that it would be accept-able.

After communicating his enthusiasm over the good news to his parents, he received a typical reply from his father: "But seriously we are glad because you are glad. It cheers us all to know when you are happy. We cannot fully enter into your feelings because we cannot see how you would be greatly benefitted, but we all congratulate you nevertheless & trust your fondest hopes may be realized and may God add his blessing to your efforts." [37] Fortu-nately, Ridgely was not discouraged by these letters from home.

There is no doubt, however, that the appearance of his new mentor, Edmund Clarence Stedman, was of great assistance to him. This new friend was a successful New York stockbroker who was also an influential poet and critic, and his career was a fasci-natingly checkered one. Having been asked to leave Yale because of his excessive interest in wine, women, and song, Stedman be-came a newspaper editor in Connecticut, but he later left for the big city. His early satirical poetry earned him some success and a lawsuit, but he later became one of the major powers in late nine-teenth-century poetry. His own work was decidedly Victorian in style and content and has gone the way of all such work, but his verse was very successful in his own time. He is now best remembered for his work as editor and critic, having edited the ten-volume edition of the works of Edgar Allan Poe in 1895 in collaboration with George E. Woodberry and having produced *A Victorian Anthology* (1895) and *An American Anthology: 1787–1900* (1900), both of which were to be found on most American bookshelves at the turn of the century. Stedman was known to be generous to young artists and to have worked "to promote the prestige of literature and alleviate the hard lot of authors." [38] He was one of the founders of the Authors' Club and also one of the presidents of the National Institute of Arts and Letters.

Just how Torrence met Stedman is an interesting story in itself and is best told in his own words:

Yesterday afternoon was my half holiday so I took a New York Central train & went up to Lawrence Park, N. Y. where E. C. Stedman lives. I went, of course to show him my mss. if possible. I arrived at the house about four o'clock & was told by the maid at the door that Mr. Stedman would not return from his Wall St. office until evening. I was sadly disappointed but finally mustered up courage to ask if any of his secretaries were in. I was told that the last one had just left the house, I then asked if I could leave a note for Mr. Stedman & was told that I could & just as I stepped in the door I met a lady who was just going out who turned out to be a secretary. The maid had been mistaken. After a half hour's conversation & by dint of hard argument I persuaded the secretary to agree to lay the mss. on Mr. Stedman's desk in a place where he would see it on his return. She at first positively declined to bother Mr. Stedman with it at all because she said he was constantly beseiged in like manner by innumerable authors. But I first persuaded her to at least deign to glance at the mss. herself and after she had done so rather carefully she agreed to keep it. That was all. I then went back to town extremely well satisfied with the afternoon's work and had faint hopes of *some day* hearing some praise from Mr. Stedman. But lo & behold *this very afternoon* who should come to the library but a lady who came she said "in behalf of Mr. Stedman" to invite me up to spend the afternoon tomorrow. She then went on to say that I ought to consider myself greatly flattered. That it was more than Mr. Stedman had ever done before for a young author. She said he had come home last night at midnight tired & sleepy and had seen my mss. lying on his table. He picked it up to see what it was, undertook to read a few numbers & finally sat down & read it through, she said he told them at the breakfast table this morning that it was very few books that could force him to commence them & finish them after midnight but that this one had done so. She told me that I had a chance to make a very near and dear friend out of Mr. Stedman & that she would advise me to stick by him. I certainly told her I would do so. So, my Darlings, I now have secured the high praise and soon hope to secure the intimate friendship of the most powerful & influential & able critic and man of letters in America.[39]

This invitation opened a whole new world for the ambitious young man from Xenia, and his first meeting with the poet was one of the most important moments of his life. His record of this auspicious event conveys not only the facts but also the excitement the young man felt at this meeting with a master:

He greeted me very courteously and said that he would at least take an hour going over and talking over the Bidpai. So we started in. He first asked me about myself and my struggles here during the past three years. When I told him of how I had worked along on $30 per mo. and how before that I was five mo. hunting a job & all about it he said: "Good, that was good for you, you needed to have the iron enter your soul a bit; it didn't hurt you a bit, now did it?" "Why" said he "my case was lots worse than yours, I entered Yale & was fired at the end of two years for having been drunk during almost the whole of those two years, I came to New York & it was *five* years instead of three that I worked in absolute dark and obscurity & had a wife & child besides." Well, after talking a while in a most beautiful & fatherly manner to me, we took up the Bidpai. "Now" said he "you tell me the truth about this poem, is it yours or Bidpai's?" I told him frankly that about 30 of the 120 had been suggested by Bidpai & that the rest was made up out of my head in fact bogus. But, I went on, of course I mustn't let the publishers know that. "Why not?" said he. "Why," said I, "they wouldn't take it." "Indeed they *will* take it," said he, "we'll see that they take it and it's all the better that the poem is your own instead of a real translation." "Now," said he, "my frank critical opinion is that it is a *very* great and noble poem. . . . I want to give you a boost that will set you where you deserve for having written this. . . . An old man likes things with flesh & blood in them & this certainly has it." . . . Well the poem occupied us for two hours, then we began to talk

& he certainly was fascinating, we became fast friends immediately. . . . The old poet does not seem to be much over fifty, his eyes are sharp & bright & he is vigorous as a young blood.[40]

From this point on, Stedman assumed a major role in Torrence's life, both artistically and socially. He gave Torrence a completely new social orientation and the introductions needed for his work to reach publication. Through Torrence's participation in Stedman's "circle," he met the people who were to be his closest friends in later years. Stedman's charming colonial house, Laura, in the glamorous artists' colony near Bronxville, replaced Xenia as the *locus* for Torrence.

There is little doubt that the secure beliefs of his new friend and adviser gave Torrence more confidence in his resistance to the values of Xenia. Stedman was a man who was both a material and an artistic success, but his outlook on life was far from that of an Ohio Presbyterian. Of course, the one value common to the world of Torrence's parents and to that of Stedman and his associates was material success. It is important to note, however, that Stedman's wealth did not come from his writings but from his business dealings. Torrence began to see that his fortune, too, would have to come from a different source than his pen: "[Poetry] will not bring me cash directly. It has led me into a society where in a year or so if I keep my health I will marry not only money but lots of it and so in the end I will have not only fame & influence but also the filthy lucre that was to be the chief end of learning arithmetic. The easiest thing in the world is to marry an heiress." [41]

This aim may seem cynical; but Torrence, whose charm appealed to women, was beginning to realize the possibilities of his relationships with his wealthy and influential acquaintances. These sentiments were to recur again and again in his correspondence with his family, not only with regard to marriage, but also friendships: "When I meet a man whom I think it is worthwhile to know, I immediately make such a friend out of him that he will do anything in his power for me. I have found that the best thing to possess in order to get along in this town is influence." [42] At first glance these statements might seem like excuses for living a more frivolous life than his parents would condone. Nevertheless, they provide an interesting commentary upon his growing participation in the affairs of New York society and upon his almost cynical understanding of the ways of the world.

Stedman's success made him respectable as a poet; but his poetry too, as indicated earlier, was in keeping with the artistic tastes of the Gilded Age. In his essays, particularly in the Turnbull lectures, *The Nature and Elements of Poetry* (1892), Stedman emerged as an opponent of Realism; for Realism, which only treats things that are seen, ignores the "Ideal," which completes truth. What Stedman felt the poet needed was an esthetic idealism, one transcending reality in a search for, and depiction of, beauty. Such statements codified the goals of the estheticism that was beginning to feel the slings and arrows of the Realists and Naturalists. At the time that Torrence met Stedman, however, he was one of the most influential figures of the literary "establishment," and his type of poetry still had a large following.

During the next few months, Stedman helped Torrence revise the Bidpai poems so that they would meet the approval of Small, Maynard. At the same time, Stedman did all that he could to see that the publisher would accept Torrence's work. As a result, Torrence received notification of acceptance on May 26, 1899, and began making the final revisions. At Stedman's insistence, he had worded the title so that the reader would realize that the poems were his and not really translations of Bidpai. The hundred poems finally appeared as *The House of a Hundred Lights: A Psalm of Experience After Reading a Couplet of Bidpai;* and, of course, the volume was dedicated to Stedman.

The final title gives a good description of what the poems actually are. A good number of the poems are of Torrence's own invention, though they are presented in the couplet form of the homilies of Bidpai. The poems are "adaptations" only in the sense that Torrence took the general idea of the couplet as the basis for his own poem. For instance, a couplet of Bidpai that can be translated, "All men understand the speech of sorrow," was adapted to:

> In all the languages of the earth
> in which the human kind confer,
> The Master-Speaker is the tear
> it is the Great Philosopher.[43]

Or the Bidpai's "I feel that I can serve in humble circumstances
as well as great ones," becomes:

> Whether I be a flower for the
> Great Gard'ner's nostrils I care not.
> Mayhap I'll be the stick of wood
> That feeds the fire to boil His pot.

As the book developed, Torrence's interest turned more and more
toward molding the verses in a humorous vein rather than in the
more didactic tone of the original Bidpai.

Finally, in November, 1899, Small, Maynard, and Company released *The House of a Hundred Lights* in a fancy green volume
decorated with gold. The edition of seven hundred and fifty copies
was not inconspicuous, for it aroused a great deal of critical
enthusiasm. Another Princetonian, Booth Tarkington, was one of
its first admirers. In a review of the work, he wrote, "The House
of a Hundred Lights is worth reading and worth keeping to read
again. It is a book for winter twilight, to be read by the fireside,
perhaps pulling at a pipe between stanzas, with the quick rumina-
tion it inspires." [44] The anonymous critic for the New York *Tribune* wrote, "Mr. Torrence aims at a fearless expression of the
truth, but he writes with a certain spirit of youth and courage,
with a certain grace of form, and hence 'The House of a Hundred
Lights' contains some interesting, beguiling verses. His work reflects a kind of common sense, practicality coloured by imagination." [45] Of course, not all the reviews were favorable, and invidi-
ous comparisons with the *Rubaiyat* occurred often, as in this judgment in *The Critic:* "It has some good lines, but not so many as
there are in the *Rubaiyat*. It will be time to read it when you
know Omar by heart." [46]

The House of a Hundred Lights, like Torrence's earlier poems,
is an eclectic work. It was clearly influenced by the *Rubaiyat*, but
to limit our discussion to this one obvious area would be to over-
simplify. Although Torrence says little about his reasons for writing the poems other than his fascination with the Bidpai works,
one can see certain intentions in the completed work. There is
little doubt that he was as eager for popular as for artistic success,
and we can see the elements of many popular works here. Torrence's fascination with the similarity between the Bidpai and

American "horse sense" was obviously one of his prime motivations. The Bidpai translations were an ideal medium for the type of homely philosophy that had been so successful in the work of the "Fireside Poets." We cannot help but notice the similarity of the more serious verses to the poems Whittier had written a generation before:

> But, by all thy nature's weakness,
>   Hidden faults and follies known,
> Be thou, in rebuking evil,
>   Conscious of thy own.[47]

We do not have to go that far back, however, for examples of the type of simple, didactic verse that constitutes a large part of *The House of a Hundred Lights*. John B. Tabb, a Baltimore priest and teacher, wrote verse of this kind, such as "Prejudice" (1894):

> A leaf may hide the largest star
>   From love's uplifted eye;
> A mote of prejudice out-bar
>   A world of Charity.[48]

Canadian-born Bliss Carman had achieved success with similar verses during the 1890's:

> And still in the honest working world,
>   With posture and hint and smirk,
> The sons of the devil are standing by
>   While man does all the work.[49]

These poems were aimed at a wider audience than was sought by the more hedonistic verse of the period. They might be called middle-class poetry, for want of a better term. Their intent is not wholly esthetic, nor is it in any way revolutionary; rather it is didactic, reiterating truisms in as charming a manner as possible. It is not surprising that Small, Maynard, which had done so well with the homely philosophy of "Mr. Dooley," was eager to publish Torrence's volume. We can see that Torrence's stanzas are far closer to the work of the "middle-class poets" than they are to the Epicureanism of *The Rubaiyat*, especially in the more serious stanzas, such as the following:

> Man's life is like a tide that weaves
>   the sea within its daily web
> It rises, surges, swells and grows,
>   —a pause—then comes the evening ebb.
>
> ....
>
> What! doubt the Master Workman's hand
>   because fleshly ills increase?
> No; for there still remains one chance
>   that I am not His Masterpiece.

If the serious stanzas are more American than Eastern, we can find even fewer traces of the Eastern in the lighter verses, such as this one in which the humorous sentiments have a distinctly Yankee flavor:

> In all the undertakings I
>   have entered in, my stratagem
> Has been to widen carefully
>   some gap for getting out of them.

There is a good deal of variety among the poems of *The House of a Hundred Lights*. In addition to the bits of worldly philosophy and humor, Torrence freely expresses his interest in more Romantic verse. Unfortunately, these all too often resemble the magazine verse of the time:

> And Maiden, should these bitter tears
> You shed be burdensome, know this:
> There is a cure worth all the pain,
> —Tonight—beneath the moon—a kiss.

Or:

> Girl, when he gives you kisses twain,
> Use one, and let the other stay;
> And hoard it, for moons die, red fades,
> And you may need a kiss—some day.

If the verses contained in *The House of a Hundred Lights* have any major flaw, it is that they are typical of the verse of their day;

for Torrence is a too adept student of Stedman and his colleagues. They are too clearly a part of what one critic has called "the school of gossamer and old gauze." Unfortunately, given Torrence's background, there were no other models to which he could have turned. With its arch verses in the style of a bygone era, its self-conscious use of archaisms, and the ornate, heavily gilded covers, *The House of a Hundred Lights* seems to exemplify all that is wrong with the poetry of the Genteel Tradition, but for a young man educated in this tradition and eager for success in a field in which conservatism is the profitable stance, Torrence's first volume is a noteworthy beginning. This was the work of a poet determined to win his audience, and while the poems show little innovation, they are proof that Torrence had mastered the tools of his trade. In a few short years he had become more than comfortable within the style of his time. It was time now for new, more exciting conquests.

CHAPTER 2

The New Woman and
The Seven Cities of Gold

I do hope that in our next incarnation
we can be lovers again—and *that* time,
have enough more star-dust, in me, to
bring it off.

Zona Gale to R. T.[1]

Into this world where life is born of
light
I, Shadow, have been sent to bring you
peace,
To make you wise; within my tragic
themes,
Lost Love, A Sullen Will, Dead Hope
and Dread
You shall find balm, pleasant with
secret nard,
To heal your discontent, for all men
know
That he for whom noon's brightest
radiance glows
Is he who waked and shuddered at
midnight.

Prologue to *El Dorado* [2]

THE beginning of the twentieth century found young poet
Ridgely Torrence a very different person from the callow
youth who had moved to the big city three years earlier. His
strong but undirected interest in writing had grown into a real
dedication to poetry. He was published; his first volume had received a good deal of critical acclaim; and he had an influential
sponsor in Edmund Clarence Stedman. Most important to the de-

velopment of his personality, he was financially independent of his family—for the time being at least. The promises he had made to himself and to his family were beginning to be fulfilled.

In November, 1898, Torrence had been transferred from the Astor Library to the Lenox Library at Fifth Avenue and Seventieth Street, where he and a Mr. Gillis were in charge of the American music and genealogies section. While this transfer represented a nominal promotion, Torrence's meager salary (he began at a salary of twenty-five dollars a month) did not improve appreciably, and the job was demanding because many women with social aspirations devoted many hours to researching their family history in search of respectable ancestors. At the time Torrence was transferred, Theodore Dreiser, an acquaintance, tried to get Torrence a job on the editorial staff of *Ainslee's Magazine,* but nothing came of it. In March, 1900, Torrence was transferred back to the Astor to classify and arrange the holdings in English literature—a task more in keeping with the young poet's interests.

If *The House of a Hundred Lights* had earned Torrence more critical recognition than public acclaim, Torrence's work was certainly brought to the public's attention through its inclusion in Stedman's *An American Anthology: 1787–1900.*[3] His contribution, consisting of excerpts from *The House of a Hundred Lights,* filled only part of two pages, but the honor of being included at all was considerable. Stedman was at the time the most influential figure in American poetry, and his selection of American poets for the anthology was considered to represent the best American poetry of the past century. Stedman's judgment was so highly respected by the general reading public that the anthology was a "best seller." Because of this fact, the inclusion of the work of Torrence, then only twenty-five, could not help but be an important stepping-stone for his career.

The center of Torrence's social life was the Stedman home in Bronxville, and it was there that he met Edwin Arlington Robinson on May 20, 1900. Torrence's initial impression of Robinson is evidence of the high esteem he had for the writer of *The Children of the Night,* an esteem that would form the basis of a friendship that lasted until Robinson's death: "He is very companionable, a scholar and gentleman I think. He has faith in himself as a poet and says he's going to keep on writing. I wish I could fix some of his fixity of effort and belief into my own life." [4] After talking after dinner at Stedman's, Torrence and Robinson took the train back to New York City together and talked at Robinson's flat until the early hours of the morning.

Robinson's biographer, Herman Hagedorn, a friend of both poets, makes some interesting observations about the meeting of these two young poets; especially interesting is his description of Torrence at this time: "Robinson was unprepared for this sprightly, mischievous being, this incarnation of youth, so individual, yet so free of pose, so fluid, so witty, so imaginative, yet so honest, and so loyal. He was outwardly almost the complete antithesis to Robinson, a social being to his fingertips, picking adventure from every bush; a fountain of gracefully rising and falling entertainment, giving himself with careless generosity, yet, like Robinson wholly self-sustaining; unpossessed and unpossessable." [5] Torrence's outward gaiety and energy may have made him seem to be the exact opposite of the timid, reserved Maine poet, but the two men were drawn together by their love for their art and the tenderness they both felt toward the people with whom they were brought into contact.

During this period, Torrence was also continuing his experiments with poetic form. In the spring of 1900, he devoted a good deal of time to the creation of a set of poems entitled "The Odour Lute." Torrence's interest in these short stanzas was to explore the poetic possibilities of vowel sounds that are associated with certain colors. Each stanza explores the sound and suggestions of a color:

The Odour Lute[6]
I
(Blue)

Beauty to illumine
Music purely human
In Eden put a lute of bloom
Through whose runic loom
Perfumes, loosened, blew
To a wooing fluent tune
Soothing the cerulean noon
With a fugue of dew.

II
(Red)

When Hesper trembled in the west
To gem the crescent's empty shell
Then, gently pensive as a bell
The scented heaven led the rest
With splendid denser heavier breath
That wept and ebbed as though it bled
Quenching yet, the legend said
Every dreaded knell of death.

III
(White)

By night a tide of shining lyres
Elided quiet for a time
By a final mighty chime
While inspired with wilder fire
A bright choir like a blind
And writhing finite mind
Sighing like gliding viols
Died as smiles die
To sighs and silences behind
The sky.

IV
(Purple)

Yearning, murmurous nocturnes
Stirred with Myrrh the ferns.
(Earth's first verdures were
Mercy and Myrrh)
Perturbed with urgent scourge and hurled
To burden earth with curse deferred
The furtive serpent lurked and heard
The worship of the virgin world.

V
(Green)

Between each leaf sleep
Concealed a peaceful dream
The fevered legion breezes ceased to weep
And grief to be the theme.
Even the Pleides agleam

> Sweeter secrets seemed to keep
> Beneath the deepening evening east
> The fleeting paean ceased.

It would be interesting to discover the reason Torrence wrote these poems at this time. He wrote his parents that "It is something that has never been done in English or any other language so Stedman says," [7] which suggests that the poems were written without any knowledge of similar work by the French *Symbolistes*. Stedman was a great admirer of Poe, and it may be that a study of the American poet and his use of sound for its expressive qualities led Torrence to try his hand at this technique. It is surprising, however, that Stedman did not note the kinship with the *Symbolistes*. Possibly he was ignorant of Baudelaire's theory that "every colour, sound, odour . . . is in some way bound up with an equivalent in each of the other fields." [8]

Interesting, too, is Torrence's own judgment of this work: "I shall not continue with such experiments for it is after all only music and only of interest to specialists. My creed of art is to write poetry that above all *says something*, that gives men something to chew on. To write poetry for mere music is like a traveller that stays forever in some pleasant inn by the roadside instead of pushing on to his journey's end." [9] His desire to write poetry that "says something" demonstrates a dissatisfaction with the type of hedonistic verse prominent during the last decade of the nineteenth century—and supported by Stedman—and his statement that such work is "only music" would have distressed his contemporaries in France. The didactic impulse, the desire to give his readers "something to chew on," remained with him throughout his career.

Surprisingly enough, Torrence's interest took a new turn during the spring of 1900. As he wrote his parents, "I am not devoting myself to little things that will bring in an immediate return but am working hard at plays and throwing all my energy in that direction except of course a book of poems that I keep going on the side." [10] His interest was in creating a poetic drama because "There is a better chance now for the poetic drama than there has been for three hundred years." [11] Torrence already had chosen his subject for his first attempt in this area: "I shall probably call mine 'El Dorado.' It is to be based on the search for the Seven Golden Cities of Cibola or El Dorado which were reported to be in Arizona and which turned out to be Pueblo and Casa Grand." [12]

In the summer Torrence was called home because of an accident his sister had had, and he was forced to prolong his stay because of his own respiratory ailment. The period of convalescence gave him the opportunity to work extensively on his play. As he wrote Josephine Preston Peabody, whom he had met through Robinson: "I have been working a good deal on my 'El Dorado' play, the first I have ever done on it in real earnest and the most diligent work I have ever put on anything thus far in my brief career. I think I have just wakened out of boyhood and if I am going to do any harm to the universe I may as well begin." [13] And, in respect to the work Torrence was writing, we cannot underestimate the importance of these two poet-friends, Edwin Arlington Robinson and Josephine Preston Peabody, at this stage of Torrence's life and career. Robinson, the lonely young man from Gardiner, Maine, had left Harvard for financial reasons in 1893, but he had returned to Cambridge to work in 1898. At that time he became close friends with Josephine Preston Peabody, then twenty-four, a former student at Radcliffe. Through Miss Peabody, Robinson, too, became friends with the brilliant Harvard poet and teacher, William Vaughn Moody.

What is important here is the interest that all of these poets had in the possibilities of poetic drama. At the time Robinson became a friend of Miss Peabody, she was beginning to work on her verse-tragedy, *Marlowe,* a piece that was typical of the work of the first decade of her career.[14] *Marlowe* was obviously closely modeled on Elizabethan drama. Its setting was the England of Marlowe's period, and the action depicted a romanticized account of the events leading to Marlowe's violent death. She evinces no interest in the creation of an American form; instead, the intent seems to be merely the reascendance of blank verse as the dramatic medium. Miss Peabody uses the form well, but the play remains an imitation of Elizabethan drama rather than a modern play using the medium of blank verse. The depiction of life in a bawdy Elizabethan tavern may hold some interest, but there is no dramatic conflict within this elaborate setting.

While *Marlowe* is a failure, it is important as an example of the resurgence of interest in verse as a dramatic medium. There is little doubt that William Vaughn Moody provided the impetus for this concern. In 1897, the year in which Miss Peabody began *Mar-*

lowe, Moody began his first verse drama, *The Masque of Judgment.* Where Miss Peabody's model was the Elizabethan drama, it is obvious that Moody was most influenced by Greek drama and such Romantic adaptions as Shelley's *Prometheus Unbound.* Moody had American precedents to follow in Richard Hovey's masque, *The Quest of Merlin,* and in Bayard Taylor's allegory, *The Masque of the Gods.* Miss Peabody's play was meant to be performed, but this first effort of Moody was obviously closet drama—a poem in dramatic form rather than a drama in verse.

Nonetheless, Moody's later work attests to his deep interest in poetic drama. In 1904, he wrote Percy MacKaye that "I am heart and soul dedicated to the conviction that modern life can be presented on the stage in the poetic mediums and adequately presented only in that manner." [15] It is no surprise, then, that Moody's interest infected Robinson and Torrence. Although Robinson's two attempts at drama were made several years later, he wrote Torrence, at this time, in reply to Torrence's announcement that he was writing a play: "I believe verse to be the only proper form for a play [if it is] to be great." [16]

Much work, then, was done on *El Dorado* during Torrence's stay in Xenia; and the fruits of his labors caused him to have high hopes for the play. A letter to Miss Peabody is evidence of this spirit: "But I really am getting enthusiastic about the play. I have changed it completely from the poor skeleton I gave you of it. The plot is entirely changed and I have one that is really ripping, I think. There is action without end in it, so much that I have to steer clear of melodrama constantly." [17] Upon his return to New York, he again sought Stedman's advice and assistance; and he was delighted when Stedman agreed that the play should be published before it was produced.

After the hunt for a publisher began in earnest, the manuscript was rejected a number of times before a helpful acquaintance was introduced to Torrence at Stedman's home: Lord Paget, a young man who had invested a lot of money in John Lane's publishing house and who had thus bought himself the job of literary representative in America for Lane. When Torrence showed Paget his manuscript, Paget agreed to do all he could to get it accepted. It must have been something of an honor for Torrence to consider the idea of his work's being published by John Lane, for Lane and his firm were champions of the poets of the 1890's. Lane not only published the work of Richard Le Gallienne and Francis Thompson's *The Hound of Heaven,* but also published, as well as helped found, *The Yellow Book,* the battleground of the real masters of the English *fin de siècle.* Lane rejected the manuscript of *El Dorado* early in 1903; and it was a full year after Torrence's meeting with Paget in June, 1902, before the Englishman's influence showed the desired result.

I *First and Second Love*

It was almost two years between the completion of *El Dorado* and its publication, but during that time Torrence's life was very full. His work at the library continued, although he was never happy with the job. Despite his slender income, he continued to aspire to social position and enjoyed being something of a lady's man. Moreover, his acquaintance with Stedman and his friends was supplemented by his acquaintance with other contemporary poets. Chief among these was Edwin Markham who lived at this time on Staten Island. Markham, a San Francisco school teacher and writer of newspaper verse, achieved nationwide acclaim after "The Man with the Hoe" was published in the San Francisco *Examiner* on January 15, 1899. Because of its concern with the plight of the poor, it was widely hailed, and it reached a far greater audience than most poems of the time. Certainly Markham would be one poet of whom Torrence's parents would approve. While Torrence did not feel the reverence for Markham that he felt for Stedman, he was fond of the earthy poet. When Torrence returned from a visit to Xenia early in 1901, Markham asked him to assist him in editing an anthology of memorial poems for *McClure's.* Although Torrence seemed enthusiastic about the project, it never materialized.

It is a long way from Xenia to New York, and Torrence had built a new world for himself in the metropolis, but his ties to his parents were still very close. He still wrote them twice a week, and he still felt called upon to justify his literary activity and his way of life. There can be no doubt of his devotion to his family, but it also seems clear that their lack of understanding of his work was a constant source of frustration. Added to this frustration were the feelings of inadequacy engendered by the difficulty of securing a publisher for *El Dorado* and the long period of waiting before he saw it in print. Up to this time, Torrence seemed able to keep his spirits through any crisis; but his dream of success seemed less and less attainable.

His correspondence with poetess Josephine Preston Peabody served as a bolster to his flagging spirits and provided a good deal of inspiration, but not all his friendships with the young ladies of his circle were as platonic as his friendship with Miss Peabody. In December, 1901, Torrence wrote his parents of the engagement of Stedman's granddaughter, Laura; and he added that Laura had told him that she would rather have married him. At this time he was courting Emily Spackman, daughter of a director of the Dime Savings Bank and treasurer of the Mexican Central Railroad— Torrence had made a point of looking up her father in the *Directory of Directors*. Still, marriage did not seem to be an imperative: "Yes, I am pretty thoroughly in love with Emily. I don't know, I can't tell what time may bring but we may decide to get married one of these days. And yet now that I have written that down, I shrink from the thought of it. It seems a horribly commonplace thing for her and me to do. I guess on second thought we won't." [18]

His ardor cooled to an even lower temperature during the next month: "She isn't a bit of a gusher but she always means what she says. I really think I would marry her if I didn't firmly believe I could do better when I got a little older and more of a reputation." [19] Whether or not Torrence really believed it, he certainly wanted to give his parents the impression that his marriage would be a practical one designed to solve all his economic problems. As a matter of fact, this pose—if it was that—provided a justification for his social life: "You can bet your bottom dollar that if I had been born with any money I wouldn't fool with society for a second." [20]

Torrence's association with society, then, was merely a means of achieving material success—or so he wanted his parents to believe. Whether or not his motivation was so totally opportunistic is open to question, but it is clear that he was proud of his social conquests: "I pride myself on one thing and that is that I don't know any man who is able to go in as good society as I do for less than ten thousand a year and I do it on my face and the inside of my head alone, certainly not on the inside of my pocket or anybody's for that matter." [21]

Whatever his motivation, his infatuation for Emily Spackman, brief as it was, was probably the inspiration for his poem "The Entreaty," which was written in the late fall of 1901 and published in the October, 1902, issue of *The Smart Set.* Unlike Torrence's previous verse, this is a straightforward love poem, more emotional than his earlier work, but not devoid of many of his characteristic traits. It is not surprising to find the emphasis on color evident previously in "The Odour Lute" or the use of Classical allusion. The rhetorical devices used to convey the emotion are overdone in the manner of the poets of the previous decade, but the poem does mark a new smoothness and freedom in Torrence's expression. It does not give the impression of contrivance to the same extent as his earlier work:

> You make me dream of gold asleep.
>> What strands await me, uncaressed?
>> What molten breaths, what heats unguessed
> Are coiled for me, deep under deep.
> *And all the moons that were in me awake breathlessly and beam*
>> *to you:*
> *And all the seas that stir in me throb up, like stars, and stream*
>> *to you.*
>
> You make me dream of white. No air
>> Was there upon your face or breast;
>> No storm, no hue, but only rest,
> And grief went quiet as a prayer.
> *Troy leapt—it sank, and must again, and the night brood on the*
>> *meres of it;*
> *Fierce Babylon is dust again, its kisses with the tears of it.*
>
> You make me dream of red. The room
>> Pulsed all about us, like a flame;
>> The hour! the voices—with them came
> The crimson pressages of doom.
> *O sweet, I want the whole of you—that gold which is a part of*
>> *you,*
> *The dew which is the soul of you, the fire which is the heart of*
>> *you!* [22]

The acceptance of "The Entreaty" by *The Smart Set* gave Torrence a new interest in magazines as a means of security: "I have about decided to write steadily for the magazines. I think I could make much money by it." [23] Yet he still felt that to do such work was demeaning for a serious writer.

Meanwhile, Emily Spackman faded out of the picture, and Zona Gale began to play a prominent part in the young poet's life. Born in Portage, Wisconsin, in 1874 and graduated from the University of Wisconsin, the beautiful young writer came to New York to join the staff of the *Evening World* after a number of years on Milwaukee newspapers. Miss Gale, who considered herself a "New Woman," spent much of her life in various political movements, including woman's suffrage. In 1921 she won the Pulitzer Prize for her play, *Miss Lulu Bett.* The Zona Gale who entered Torrence's life in 1902, however, was an ambitious young journalist who in July, 1902, became E. C. Stedman's secretary. Torrence's love for "the prize beauty," as he called her in one letter, did not take long to manifest itself. By June, he seems to have been smitten, especially after one Shakespearean evening when he climbed up the lattice work onto the balcony of Miss Gale's room in Stedman's house to offer protestations of his love.

As we might expect, Torrence catalogued every phase of their courtship in his letters to his family—in addition to sending her letters home. The letters often read like magazine fiction, as does this account of an evening walk: "So we plunged into the wilderness and succeeded in getting lost in the darkness. Then a most terrific thunder storm came up and we took refuge in the ruins of a rustic summer house. The lightning and thunder went off simultaneously like cannon seemingly around us. It was very wild and beautiful and was of course made doubly enchanting by having this stunningly beautiful girl clinging so desparately to me. Of course I didn't let such an opportunity go by without making desparate love to her in order to complete the scene. It beat any written romance." [24]

Zona was equally enamoured, as her poem, "You," demonstrates; for the "you" is obviously Torrence:

> No more for me the ways of life that lead
> Through curtained wood and down the dim lit lane;
> No more the call of shadows, petal shaped,
> Caught in dim colored cups that fade and feed
> The earth, wistful of earth. And spread in vain
> Are seed sown webs, whitening the new-drenched way.

But always you; the sun-lamped lane and you!
The woods—and you! Shadows that rock all day
In painted bells—and you! Always your face
Is on the hills and in the nets of dew
Hung on gray leaves. Ah, all the dream-steeped way
Is wild with you! For I have seen your face.[25]

Despite the fact that the two young writers were obviously much attached to each other, Torrence never quite trusted Zona Gale. It was exciting to know an "emancipated" woman, but she was not the type of girl one married: "I have to laugh at your telling me to marry a girl like Zona Gale. She would be as unfaithful a creature as you could possibly get hold of." [26] He did love Zona Gale, but wealthy Emily Spackman still represented the type of girl he wished to marry: "What would you say if I was to marry Emily before a year from now? It isn't improbable. If I did I would go in the offices of the Mexican Central Railroad of which Mr. Spackman is a large owner. Emily thinks it would be just the place. She has about a hundred thousand dollars worth of stock in the R. R. herself." [27] Torrence's parents were baffled by their son's strange fickleness. We cannot but feel that his mother's reaction was justified: "I do wish you would school yourself to be not quite so promiscuous in your attentions. I fear you will suffer for it some day." [28]

Torrence's parents did not have to worry long, for love soon conquered practicality: Zona became the whole object of Torrence's affections, and he decided to marry her if and when his writing gave him some financial security. That Torrence loved Zona cannot be doubted, but there was still a gnawing doubt that he could not overcome. On one day he wanted to marry her; on another, he would write his parents that "I wouldn't marry her if she were the last woman on earth. Although we are good friends." [29] There was enough of Torrence's Calvinistic background in him to make him suspicious of a woman who had done anything immoral. Zona had had a clandestine affair with Richard Le Gallienne, a married man, before meeting Torrence. She had completely severed relations with him when she became aware of her feelings for Torrence; but, one day in the spring of 1901 when Le Gallienne visited Zona in her apartment, Torrence came to call and found him there; and, despite Zona's protestations of innocence, he was sure that he had been betrayed. He felt that he could never trust Zona again.

This unfortunate incident led to a parting that was long and painful for both parties. In August, Torrence visited the distressed girl in Wisconsin; but the feelings of distrust could not be overcome. He even wrote Zona's confidante, the opera singer Mme Conover, and told her the whole story—an action that hurt Zona terribly and impelled her to write a long letter to explain her feelings for Torrence: "You had for me, as I for you, the perfect appreciation of the outward semblance of things—and you had in addition more than I had ever dreamed of the sense of things, of the world, or wonder—and you made me self conscious; you taught me understanding." [30] But there was also a negative side to her feelings about Torrence: "I knew of your unreliability, I knew from you and the others that you were irresponsible—I put it all together and thought of you as an adorable companion too—but utterly impossible as a lover because you had no least stability." [31] It is hard to say who was ultimately responsible for the end of what should have been a perfect romance. We are prone to ascribe most of the blame to Torrence's lack of trust in Zona. It seems that he always thought of her as a "loose woman," and no amount of feeling for her could change this idea which the unfortunate meeting with Le Gallienne merely confirmed.

There is little doubt that Torrence's love for Zona detracted from his work as a poet. In March, 1903, he wrote his parents about what was to become his next project: "I am also digging away on a play. The play is called 'Abelard and Heloise' and is the tragedy of those two lovers. Strangely enough it has never been written up & is the last great romance of history to remain thus far." [32] Despite the existence of the germinal idea, *Abelard and Heloise* waited until 1907 for publication. Meanwhile, *El Dorado* was still unpublished. During the spring of 1903, Torrence decided to resign from the library. So that he would not formally sever connections until he was sure of a new income, he obtained a leave-of-absence until October 1. Edwin Markham offered him a job as his secretary, but this did not attract him. He did accept a job writing some articles for *Success Magazine*, however, the longest of which, "The Young Men in the Government," appeared in the June, 1903, issue. Torrence considered such commercial

ventures a form of prostitution and was upset when the Xenia
Gazette heralded his contributions:

> My but did it make me tired to hear in Daddy's letter that that
> infernal Gazette had called attention to the fact that I had an
> article in Success. I was heartily ashamed of having written such
> an article and not very proud of being in Success but with un-
> erring misjudgment they light on a commonplace affair of that
> kind and give it a great write up & when El Dorado came out
> they dismissed it with the notice that I "had a book called El
> Dorado just published" . . . I suppose I could go on & produce
> books till I was black in the face and they would never notice it
> but if my picture was in the Police Gazette they would herald me
> as Xenia's greatest son.[33]

In addition to being demeaning to a serious writer, this type of
free-lance work was not lucrative enough to support a young
writer with no other source of income; and, as a result, the search
for a job continued.

II El Dorado

Finally, in late August, 1903, *El Dorado* was published in an
edition that was attractive, if not one so opulent as that provided
for *The House of a Hundred Lights:* the covers were green with
the title in gold. Although the book bore the distinguished imprint
of John Lane, "New York and London," it was printed in Boston
by the Heintzemann Press, which had also printed the first volume; and the dedication was to Torrence's parents.

There are a number of important influences on the creation of
El Dorado in addition to the interest of Torrence's friends in the
renaissance of the verse drama. Of course, the most important of
these is Elizabethan drama; and we have already seen how this
literature fascinated Josephine Preston Peabody and that there is
little doubt that her enthusiasm served as an impetus for the im-
pressionable poet. It is also true that the historical melodrama was
a popular—and therefore profitable—medium for the practical
dramatist. Torrence's friend, Percy MacKaye, was to achieve his
greatest success in this genre before the first decade of the new
century was over.

There was, however, a third very important influence on *El Dorado;* the dramas of Henrik Ibsen: "The play will, I think, be the first instance of Ibsen's influence on the romantic or Shakespearean drama. I have fused the two methods as well as I was able." [34] What Torrence seems to be after in *El Dorado* is the large-scale romantic drama, modeled upon the work of the master of this genre, William Shakespeare, but with a difference. The difference is that the traditional dramatic conflict is replaced by psychological conflict. "No one is killed and only one man dies," [35] Torrence wrote. The causes of the "tragedy" of the major characters are lodged within them as much as they are imposed from without. The basic problem with *El Dorado* is the result of this formal split; the panoramic drama does not make as effective a background for psychological drama as does the smaller-scaled drawing-room drama of Ibsen, August Strindberg, or James A. Herne, for that matter.

El Dorado is a play about a series of futile searches: the search of Coronado for the magnificent golden treasure of the Seven Cities of Cibola; that of Perth for a reunion with his son Coronado; and that of Beatrix for her love, Coronado. When Coronado is sent to find the gold, Beatrix disguises herself as a boy and follows him. She is accompanied by the old man, Perth, who has been a convict for thirty years, having been imprisoned for secretly marrying a nobleman's daughter. When they finally reach Coronado, he believes they are spies and decides to have them shot. Perth, however, saves the young man's life, knowing that it is his son; and Coronado lets them join his mission. The fourth act reveals the characters a year later on the banks of the Missouri River. Beatrix is still in disguise; and Coronado does not yet realize that the faithful old man, Perth, is his father. When dawn rises and the soldiers realize that they still have not reached their destination, they become mutinous. Coronado, despairing, tries to leap from the cliff; but he is stopped by Beatrix, who finally reveals her identity:

> Cor.   O—I believe—witness, dear God—my faith
>   That this, of truth,—is she—in very flesh!
>   And for my mighty faith take her not from me. [36]

When Beatrix leaves the scene, Perth comes on; and he hears Coronado tell of the real treasure he has found:

Perth. What new-fledged day is this within you
        That makes your every breath rise with mad wings?
        Have you found gold?
Cor.   Yes, gold more dear
        Than the good earth or the sky's gilded blue,
        Or sea-caves carven of peace have ever yielded!
Perth. Where?
Cor.   It is stored here. (*He points to his breast.*)
                    Here, beyond all sight
        Save mine!
Perth. And so at last you know—
Cor.   Know? What?
Perth. The gold that thrills within your veins, the treasure
        Unstolen by the furtive creeping years.
Cor.   The youth of which you dream? Yes, I possess it.
Perth. But I did not find it there upon the plain,
        Neither the golden earth.
Cor.   Then turn with me
        From dreams and fix your wakened eyes on day!
                        (107–8)

Torrence's theme is not an original one, although, at least in this scene, he handles it effectively. The treasure that Coronado was searching for was with him all the time: the sacrificing love offered him by Beatrix. If we can divorce from our minds the ludicrous picture of a woman who kept a helmet on with the beaver down for well over a year, we might be able to see that Beatrix becomes an idealization of the devoted, loving woman who is willing to sacrifice all for the object of her devotion. Lyman Leathers, in his dissertation on Torrence's formative years, explains the excesses of Beatrix's disguise in terms of Torrence's rather puritanical concept of propriety: "On the other hand the disguise may be associated with attitudes toward women which deemed it shameless and unladylike for Beatrix to be seen without the disguise." [37] It may be just this sort of idealization of womanhood that made it impossible for Torrence to trust fully the fidelity of Zona Gale.

In the final act of the play, Perth is dying of thirst on the summit of Thunder Mountain in New Mexico. The governor has sent a message to the effect that the voyagers will be punished if they return from their quest empty-handed. Coronado and Beatrix enter, but Perth dies before he can reveal his secret to Coronado

—that the general is his son. The final speeches of Perth are
among the most beautiful in the play:

> There had been flowers—I had thought to love a few
> Out of the dream, but now are all dreams dead.
> Poor ghosts. Yet once they seemed most real to me,
> Memories only now; the eyes that saw them
> Briefly between two shadows, now no more
> See. Nor will ever see the Garden's colours,
> . . A mist . . . a rift within the mist . . . and then . .
> The mist again and odours far away.
> . . The Sea! O wild, wide beach! Am I alone?
> The tide grows full and climbs now toward my lips;
> I will wait here. The ponderous ancient breast
> Heaves heavily its interminable sigh;
> Soon it will ebb and leave upon the sands
> No shadow of the shell that printed them.
> Nor in the thunder of sob or storm or calm,
> Or any separate wave's soliloquy,
> Will there be memory of what returned;
> So with all broken shells . . .   (130–31)

The play ends with the Epilogue by Shadow, who expresses the
mystical faith of his creator:

> Far beyond thought, One broods upon all this,
> Watching the face of many and many a world
> Whose yearning clay from time to time He dews
> With souls of men from out His infinite will.
> .   .   .   .
> He, He who dreams or watches all below,
> Waits all, withholding either blow or kiss.
> A while he suffers them to pulse or flow,
> Then reabsorbs them in those clouds of His.
>   (133)

This epilogue contains the most eloquent statement of Torrence's
own faith, but it is irrelevant. It does not really provide the
needed thematic resolution of the action of the play, nor is its
metaphysical statement relevant to what has transpired.

What we have in *El Dorado*, then, is an uneven work. As

poetry, it contains Torrence's best work thus far; for some passages, such as those quoted above, are obviously the work of a
talented poet, and the work as a whole never descends below a
level of competence. Still, it has one major weakness and that was
inherent in the work's very conception. People in twentieth-
century America do not speak Elizabethan verse, not even poets;
and the idiom is natural neither to Torrence nor to his play. Thus
much of the dialogue seems contrived and artful rather than
natural and emotionally charged. Torrence was wise in not adher-
ing rigidly to iambic pentameter, but the meter of his verse does
not always catch the natural cadence of speech:

> We have seen no gold save in the fatal sun.
> Dry flats, like those in upper hell, led on
> Only to hills more desolate with thirst. (60)

The diction, too, fails because of its artificiality. In attempting to
write dialogue that was poetic as well as dramatic, Torrence all
too often resorts to the false poetic diction of the Genteel Tradition:

> Even yesterday I questioned one returning;
> A sun-born native stripling in whom youth
> Seethes like a tide of dawn; yet he was older
> Than twice a thousand years! Each time he felt
> The withering beckoner within his blood,
> He sought Quevara and the hidden source,
> Laved his old limbs in that immortal rain
> And lived again! (82)

As drama, too, *El Dorado* is all too often wanting: the characters do not come alive, and the action is far from credible, even
within the romantic framework of the play. But the critical reception was, for the most part, favorable, despite the fact that many
felt that Torrence's gift lay in the field of poetry, not drama. Typical of these judgments is the review of "H. C." in *The Reader:*
"There is hardly a semblance of plot and no dramatic action
whatever. Therefore in considering Eldorado [*sic*] it must be
judged only as poetry, narrative, or perhaps lyrical in a way, certainly not dramatic. . . . If he will be content to keep away from
dramatic poetry and devote himself to his very evident and

marked ability in other kinds, and not publish again, it seems safe to prophesy for Mr. Torrence a very high rank among the younger poets—if not among the poets, even." [38]

The reviewer for the New York *Post* made another objection, one of the same type that was made about Miss Peabody's attempts at writing a neo-Elizabethan drama in *Marlowe:* "But though weak as drama, Mr. Torrence's volume, taken piecemeal as a set of poetic dialogues of the kind, for instance, to which Browning has accustomed us, contains some pretty good poetry. . . . There is only one fault to be found with it, as with his poetry in general. Instead of being the result of a personal transformation wrought upon his studies, it remains at best recognizably Elizabethan." [39]

There were more enthusiastic comments. Guy Carleton Lee wrote in the Los Angeles *Times* that "it is in some respects the most remarkable drama in verse that has appeared in English since the death of Robert Browning," [40] a high compliment indeed from an American critic of this period. Edith M. Thomas wrote in *The Critic* that "whether or not Mr. Torrence has fulfilled all technical dramatic requirements, all his work in this poem bears the stamp of exquisite; and the charmed reader will find therein much that fulfills the 'Shadow's promise of "balm, pleasant with the secret nard" of melancholy, mysterious poesy.'" [41]

This critical acclaim suggests that we may judge the play unfairly if we use critical standards not of its age. *El Dorado,* an ambitious play, aims at the grand scene and a language that is lofty and eloquent. It is an anachronism, but it is also the work of a good craftsman.

CHAPTER 3

The Judson Circle and
Abelard and Heloise

> I met yesterday a young chap called
> Ridgely Torrence, a very charming
> and amusing fellow, who has just
> written a five-act verse play entitled
> *Eldorado,* dealing with the Spanish
> search for the Seven Cities of Gold
> and other wonders. He says he is
> writing one on Abelard and Heloise
> for Mrs. Fiske.[1]
> —William Vaughn Moody
> to Harriet Brainerd
> December 1, 1903

I *Magazine Days*

THE publication and favorable critical reception of *El Dorado*
was not the only good fortune Torrence had upon returning
to New York in September, 1903. After years of frustration at the
Astor Library, he finally found a job that was more suited to his
interests, as the assistant editor of *The Critic,* "A Monthly Review
of Literature, Art, and Life," which Putnam's published. The editor of this attractive monthly was Jeanette L. Gilder, the sister of
Richard Watson Gilder, editor of *The Century.*

Although most of Torrence's work for *The Critic* was strictly
editorial or involved with the writing of the regular column, "The
Lounger," a cooperative section without a by-line, he did contribute two major pieces during his stay, "The Masque of Hours," a
poem published in the issue of March, 1904, and an article, "Verse
—Recent and Old" in the August, 1904, issue. The article, Torrence's first critical piece, is a comprehensive review of a number

of poetic publications, written in a highly ornate style common to many of the periodicals of the time. Of Josephine Preston Peabody's new volume, Torrence made this characteristic comment: "The perfect choice of her forms is another phase to be noted of Miss Peabody's art. She sets sail within her soul and her metres are the wind that blow her to her destined bourne, which is the temple of little secrets of great magics." [2] This sort of impressionistic criticism tells us little about the poetry but much about its emotional effect on Torrence.

"The Masque of Hours" is one of his better early poems, for it contains a much more natural flow of language than is found in the more ambitious *El Dorado*. As it is not included in any of Torrence's volumes, the work deserves reproduction here:

The Masque of Hours[3]

THE MOST HIGH VOICE:

Time, who behind the high, dark hedge of space there lurkest,
Whispering years that grow ever white as the north,
I am thy lord. Show me the thing thou workest,
Come forth!

TIME:

Lord, I have labored and breathed
On the world that Thou gavest me;
My word is a blade unsheathed,
And Death and Life are two seas
With whose waters Thou lavest me.
I dream, and upon her sweet knees
Beauty comes unto the dust.
I look, and she flushes anew;
I commanded,—holding Thy trust,
And appointed a season for dew,
And the places of shade.
And again I took Love and the sun
In my hands and a singing was made,
And the song was called Life, with Pain for its utmost chord.
Yet not I—Thou art the one,
And before Thy face Lord,
I am cold and afraid.

THE VOICE:

Thou art wise, yet hast not wrought these things alone.
Concerning thy children, thy helpers, be not mute.

Thou art a field that I have sown,
Show me thy fruit.

TIME:

Now, Breath of my Dream, upon no faltering wing
Go forth from my bosom, thy prison:
Rise, and, being arisen,
Sing!

DAWN:

Loose me, and let me come like snow.
There are three marvels I can show,
Three things that men shall ponder long:
Music where no sound seemed to pass,
Spring where the soul of Winter was,
Silence where hidden thunders throng.
My upper sweet is a star's breath,
My lower glory laughs at Death,
And all my wonder is a song.

THE MORNING HOURS:

Through no horizon's restless bound
We watch that mystery, the ground,
How the bright spirit of Godhood grows
From the long passioning of the mould.
With awe renewed we watch the old
Transfiguration of the rose,
The humble witness of the weeds,
The resurrection of the seeds;
And a flower comes, and a flower goes.

NOON:

Look, and draw near to me. Behold
How I can be both sweet and gold,
How my breast's whiteness is the land,
And the sea's smile is mine eye's blue.
It is my mouth that makes for you
Summer, and it is my hand
Shows through the snow the first-born bud.
The fury of my sudden blood
Sifts out the souls of men like sand.

THE EARLY AFTERNOON HOURS:

Life to the first lull after wine
Are we, or like a lifting vine

When it has given half its grapes.
Light is our gold and our alloy,
And day to us is like men's joy,
For some abides and much escapes.
Our sleep is brief as a child's tear,
And, waking, we still see and hear
The sound of toiling and the shapes.

THE LATE AFTERNOON HOURS:

Out of all languors of dead veins,
Out of the softness of old rains,
Time's loom has woven wings for us
Wherewith we stir not from our rest
Till all the world comes in the west
And without sound it sings for us.
Then are the vanished heard to sigh,
And in the garden-colored sky
A homing wing is murmurous.

TWILIGHT:

Beyond the dim air's uttermost deep,
Upon the outer walls of sleep
My dwelling and my dreaming is.
The wonder of me is my peace;
The pity is, my sigh's release,
—But no man's mind may compass this.
Dew heals my heart of any drouth,
And on my brow and on my mouth
Both Light and Shadow lay a kiss.

THE EVENING HOURS:

White heights whose sweetness makes them blue,
Great blues the moon makes white of hue,
A ripe star gathered like a sheaf—
These are the signs with which we veil
Sorrow and with these banners hail
Sleep; and the wisdom of all grief
Comes thus within an eyelid's ken.
So from the shoulders of all men
The sky is lifted like a leaf.

MIDNIGHT:

Look, for I have no eyes to see!
Listen! For now there seemed to be

Some world that fell across the sky.
Where are the lights that filled the void?
Where is the bloom some breath destroyed?
Within what deeps are those who die?
Only from out the empty place
For ever comes before my face
A wind, a blindness, and a cry.

THE HOURS OF DEEPEST NIGHT:
Mourners, and all who fly afraid
In the grey, soundless hollow of shade
Where the first sleep is all too late,
Come to our well without a shore
From which we draw up dew to pour
Upon the lives that we await.
But still above our agate jars
The weary shuttles of the stars
Toil at the weaving that is Fate.

The poem demonstrates the simplicity of language that was evident in the most effective passages of *El Dorado*. A brief comparison with the earlier "Astarte" shows how much Torrence has developed away from *fin de siècle* stylistic excesses. Characteristically, Torrence has devised a very rigid form for the main body of the poem—a nine-line stanza with the rhyme scheme *aabccbddb*. The result is effective in giving the stanza a strong sense of unity. Little need be said about the content of the poem, for it is reminiscent not only of the Jonsonian masque but also of the Triumphs, the spectacular allegorical paintings that one finds on the wall or ceiling of a Baroque palace. Highly ornate, the poem is quite in the grand manner.

The more mundane aspects of Torrence's tasks at *The Critic* were far from interesting, and Torrence hated the editorial work that comprised much of his job. *The Critic* had no advertising, so the main problem was spacing the photographs and illustrations which were of every conceivable size and shape, like an "intricate Chinese puzzle." [4] The more pleasant tasks, reading manuscripts and interviewing people, Torrence could dispatch with more equanimity. His writer friends certainly understood his irritation with his work, as is evidenced by Robinson's remark to Miss Peabody that, "If you have any sympathy to spare, for heaven's sake think of poor Torrence under the eye of J. L. Gilder, reading bad

manuscript from morning to night. . . ." [5] Torrence's tenure at
The Critic was cut short by a serious case of paratyphoid; and in
July, 1904, he returned to Xenia to recuperate. He was well
enough in August to go to Portage, Wisconsin, to try to effect a
reconciliation with Zona Gale, but it was of no use. He returned to
Xenia and resumed work on *Abelard and Heloise;* but, when his
physical weakness got the best of him, he was bedridden again
and sick enough for the Xenia *Gazette* to report that he was seriously ill; however, Torrence recovered sufficiently to return to
New York at the beginning of 1905. The only fruit of his stay at
Xenia was "The Inscription," written in honor of the placing of
the cornerstone of the Xenia Library Building in June, 1904. Its
only appearance in print during Torrence's lifetime was in the
Xenia *Gazette* of July 26, 1904:

> Of granite and marl we build us walls
> With iron and oak for outward furniture,
> Within are dreams. The stone may not endure.
> To one faint ash with wood the metal falls.
> The dreams remain in dim eternal halls,
> Builded of mind on mind, that do immure
> Beauty and strife and prayer, and all things pure
> Which to the soul the written page recalls.
>
> So here the lulled Greek flutes may wake some youth.
> Or one shall burn with Agamemnon's glance.
> Or watch with David by the shadowy cattle
> Biding his hour. With Portia or with Ruth
> Maids may find sisterhood, or old Romance
> Louden upon the wind and win a battle.[6]

Torrence returned to New York, once again jobless; but, after
several months of searching, he was hired by *Cosmopolitan* as
fiction editor. The *Cosmopolitan* job was less demanding than Torrence's position with *The Critic,* but it was equally as harrowing.
Torrence, who took the place of three readers on the *Cosmopolitan* staff, had to read every story submitted to the magazine and
select a number of the best from which Baily Maillard, his superior, would make the final selection. Unfortunately, Maillard was
seldom available when needed and, when finally found, would
usually make the final approval without reading the work of any

of the entrants. Despite this frustration, the job provided a decent
salary, and it allowed Torrence to work on his poetry with some
sense of financial security.

If Torrence was not devoting his time away from the magazine
to poetry, he was spending it with poets. The few leisure moments
he permitted himself were usually spent with Robinson, Moody,
and Percy MacKaye, the playwright son of actor Steele MacKaye.
These men sustained Torrence's devotion to the cause of poetic
drama:

> Last night I dined with Moody and Percy MacKaye. Moody is
> going to have his verse play put on the stage out in Chicago and
> Percy MacKaye is publishing a new verse play at the end of the
> month and a copyright performance will be given in London
> week after next. We three are the prime movers in the new
> movement for the poetic drama in this country and it is going
> to succeed. I am very anxious to get settled so that I can finish
> Abelard. I read them the scenario and they were wild about it.
> They think it can be made a big money making thing.[7]

Not only did Moody and MacKaye provide the needed inspiration, they also provided many suggestions as to how *Abelard and
Heloise* could be improved.

Although a good deal of time was spent by Torrence on dramatic work, the main project of the summer months was the completion of a new poem in time for the September issue of the *Atlantic
Monthly*. Torrence was not the only person interested in the
progress of "The Lesser Children," for his friends watched avidly
the development of the work. Robinson wrote his friend Mrs.
Laura Richards: "I have been reading Torrence's monumental
poem for the September *Atlantic*, by means of which he hopes to
leap into immortal glory and leave Moody in the shadow, swear-
ing. I don't think that he will quite do it, but he will do enough to
make some thousands of people rub their eyes." [8] After the publication of "The Lesser Children," a threnody, in the September
Atlantic, Robinson wrote Miss Peabody:

> what do you say of RT's game poem in the Atlantic. He is after
> Moody's blood, apparently, and he appears to have hypnotized
> Perry with the Xenial flow of his afflatus. Personally, I maintain
> that the Lesser Children is almost the thing—the thing Done,

with a thundering big D. But there is too much of it, and in spite
of its color and warmth, and what seems to be feeling, the picture is a bit vague. It will not stand up with Moody's Ode, I
should say, but it will come very near to doing it. R. T.'s belief
in his own power is getting to be something mountainous, and I
[am] more than half inclined to share with him in his belief.
I cannot honestly say that I ever did before, but since my return
to New York I have seen signs in him of a presumed Phoebus
Apollo, gone a little wrong, that brings me up with quick jumps.[9]

The enthusiasm of Torrence's friends was echoed in "The Con-
tributors' Club" section of the November *Atlantic* which contained a four-page piece "Mr. Torrence's Metrical Art." The essay
calls the poem, "a technical triumph in which every one who is
interested in the future of poetry and who knows how to examine
and delight in its methods and potencies must share." [10] The article describes the many variations Torrence has incorporated into
the basic iambic-pentameter structure of "Threnody." For those
who would attack Torrence for taking liberties with his meter, the
critic counters: "Indeed, there is virtually no limit to the possible
deviations of verse from the colorless normal of its form; and
these deviations—and this is the point to be emphasized—are es-
sential to English verse." [11] The article closes by stating that "there
is not heard with frequency in modern verse such an orchestra as
this which in the 'Threnody' Mr. Torrence has summoned to his
hand." [12] It is seldom that a magazine poem is followed by such a
thorough—and praiseworthy—analysis.

The poem itself is an interesting one. Torrence has forsaken the
dramatic form entirely to offer a formal lament in blank verse, but
the poem has the same sweeping lyricism that distinguished the
better passages in *El Dorado*. The topic is not of the metaphysical
sort that would have inspired Moody, reminiscent as this poem is
at times of Moody's style. Rather it is the beginning of a new
interest in writing about nature. The poem might well have been
inspired by a walk during his long illness through the rolling
countryside outside of Xenia. At any rate, we see the beginnings
of a regional poet who is interested in the concerns of his own
area. "The Lesser Children" is a lament for the animals needlessly
slaughtered by hunters. These animals not only contribute to the
beauty of nature but also maintain nature's balance and serve
man by destroying many of the harmful elements in their domain:

> Watchmen of whom our safety takes no heed;
> Swift helpers of the wind that sowed the seed
> Before the first field was or any fruit;
> Warriors against the bivouac of the weed;
> Earth's earliest ploughman for the tender root.[13]

With this subject, Torrence is finally able to integrate his technique with a theme with which he is comfortable. For the first time, we sense a subordination of craft to idea; and the idea is an aspect of what becomes the dominant theme in Torrence's later lyrics—the destructive effect on a harmonious world of man's cruelty and greed.

"The Lesser Children" is typical of the best of Torrence's work at this time. The diction is more natural than that of his earlier work, though he does not always seem comfortable with the iambic pentameter line. Once again, the vivid color imagery is particularly effective:

> Clothed on with red they were who once were white;
> Drooping, who once led armies to the sun,
> Of whom the lowly grass now topped the flight;
> In scarlet faint who once were brave in brown;
> Climbers and builders of the silent town,
> Creepers and burrowers all in crimson dye,
> Winged mysteries of song that from the sky
> Once dashed long music down.[14]

Torrence's threnody was the most important work of his career thus far, for it marks the beginning of his mastery of the lyric poems that were to be his best work. But the recognition achieved by Torrence for this poem did not diminish his interest in writing plays, an interest which was certainly sustained in part by his association with MacKaye and Moody: "We, our clique of MacKaye, Moody, and I are gradually butting into the theatrical ring and we are all working together for each other. Each one's success means that much more influence for the others." [15]

II *Recognition and New Home*

On September 1, 1906, the *Fortnightly Review* published an article by May Sinclair entitled "Three American Poets of Today." Miss Sinclair, the British novelist, had spent part of the preceding

winter in America preparing for the publication of her latest
novel, *The Divine Fire*. During that time, she seems to have done
some research into contemporary American poetry, the results of
which emerge in her article. For Miss Sinclair, Robinson, Moody,
and Torrence are the leading American poets: "They are all three
rich in imagination, but Mr. Moody is distinguished by his mastery of technique, Mr. Robinson by his psychological vision, his
powerful human quality, Mr. Torrence by his immense, if as yet
somewhat indefinite promise." [16] Of course Miss Sinclair's treatment of her subject is interesting, but what is most significant
about her article is its consideration of these three poets as the
leaders of the "new poetry" in America. Although they considered
themselves as something of a circle, the critics had not yet seen
them in that light.

Miss Sinclair's comments about the individual poets are illuminating. She credited Moody with "the cosmic imagination, the
spiritual vision to which all solid-seeming things become transpar-
ent and transitory. . . . His quality is opulence, a certain gor-
geousness that is never barbaric, owing to his power of classic
restraint." [17] If Moody is characterized by this opulence, Robinson
has "the great gift of spiritual imagination and an unerring skill
in disentangling the slender threads of thought and motive and
emotion." [18] Finally, Miss Sinclair discussed Torrence's work, principally *El Dorado*, of which she wrote: "The effect of the drama
is, on the whole, spectacular rather than orchestral; it leaves the
impression of clever grouping, of the vast movements of masses
on a splendid background. But the psychology is mainly a thing of
general terms. The characters conceal their souls under a wreath
of imagery, under phrases that are like flung flowers, till we long
for the simple half-articulate utterance of human passion." [19]

This recognition, though not wholly enthusiastic, must have
been heartening to Torrence, who was still writing *Abelard and
Heloise*, which he claims was progressing by "thirty lines *every*
day" during the spring of 1906.[20] His parents were skeptical of his
enthusiasm about the creation of poetic drama, feeling that it
would never replace the work of such popular playwrights as
Clyde Fitch in the minds of the public. Torrence could not resist
countering such an attitude: "You are mistaken about the time
that I have put in on it being lost. It was growing all the time and
if you bring such fellows as Clyde Fitch into comparison you are

still more wrong. Our school of the younger and better men are going to run Clyde Fitch off the boards. Mark my words, it will be done. Clap trap work like his will go for a while but it can't stand the test of time." [21]

As we may readily see, Torrence's hopes were high for *Abelard and Heloise*. Fortunately, they were not dampened this time by another prolonged search for a publisher. On October 27, 1906, Scribner's sent the poet its acceptance of his manuscript. This news, of course, was welcome, and it probably provided some of the motivation for Torrence's move to the Judson Hotel. This hotel at 53 Washington Square was originally built as a living quarters for young Baptist men, but the Judson family could not continue to support it and were about to close the establishment when their coachman asked if he and his wife could try to convert it to a profitable hotel. Thanks to the coachman's aptitude for business and his wife's good cooking, the venture was an unqualified success.

In addition to these attributes, the Judson quickly established a reputation of being a haven for literary people. Robert Louis Stevenson's widow had lived there, and it was rumored that Frank Norris had written *The Pit* in one of the rooms. At the same time that Torrence established residence at the Judson, Robinson took a room there. His biographer, Hermann Hagedorn, describes his and Torrence's fellow tenants:

Beside Torrence, who had moved to the hotel with him, there was a group of unusually intelligent men and women who drew out the evening meal with amusing talk. Lyman Beecher Stowe, black-haired and rosy cheeked, nephew of Henry Ward Beecher, grandson of the author of *Uncle Tom's Cabin*, was editing a precarious little hearth-and-home magazine, called *The Circle;* Olivia Howard Dunbar was free-lancing in the magazines and newspapers, writing short stories and book-reviews. There were a number of other young women, intelligent and amusing. A white-haired sprightly little matron, Mrs. Roswell G. Mason, was full of life and wit; another Mrs. Mason, a blind woman, was intellectually keen. Occasionally a third Mason, Daniel Gregory, joined the group. Nazimova, gifted and intense, touched its fringes. Moody, and more rarely, a tall lean poet with black hair and flashing eyes, Percy MacKaye came and went, and occasionally a friend of Torrence named Louis Ledoux.[22]

Louis Ledoux, one of Torrence's closest friends, was a poet with a strong interest in the civilization of Japan. The son of a wealthy metallurgical chemist, Ledoux was exceedingly generous with his money—to the good fortune of his friends.

Torrence's closest friend at the Judson was Robinson, but his relationship to the Maine poet seems almost to be that of an older brother. Torrence understood the moody poet's frequent times of depression and he often rescued him from alcohol-inspired melancholia and from neighboring saloons. Torrence's strong affection for the Maine poet may be seen in this letter to Torrence's brother: "Robinson is descended from Old Puritan stock and the iron of his ancestors seeing forever battling in him,—an alien quality, serving only to chill him and breeding melancholy as in Hawthorne: shy, melancholy, remote. To the few friends that he has, however, he reveals a wealth of intellectual delight and warm hearted ways. . . . He is a man of such exquisite sensibilities that it amounts to a painful sensitiveness." [23]

Also residing at the Judson was Olivia Howard Dunbar, and she and Torrence soon developed a close friendship. Not only was Torrence visiting Olivia in her rooms at the Judson, he had also escorted her to Cos Cob, a Connecticut village on Long Island Sound, where he and his friends spent many weekends. Torrence wrote his parents that, "She is young and pretty. Ah me." But it was not long after this first mention of Miss Dunbar that his description of her to his family was revised: "She is older than I am and just a good friend of mine. No nonsense." [24] Whatever their relationship was at this time, Torrence and Miss Dunbar became man and wife eight years later.

If Torrence found a happy, inspiring milieu with the small, closely knit circle of artists at the Judson, his colleagues were more than appreciative of his presence. Daniel Gregory Mason, the composer and musicologist, recorded his memories of the evenings at the Judson in his memoir, *Music In Our Time and Other Reminiscences* (1938). Central to the memory of those experiences was Torrence himself:

> At our evening gatherings in the Judson the chief entertainer was always Ridgely Torrence. Ridgely was tall, thin, and very blonde. Singularly penetrating eyes gave to the long lean face under his

high forehead an effect of spirituality, almost aesceticism. . . .
He selected his words with the deliberation of a fastidious writer,
and had a way sometimes of under-emphasizing, almost slurring
over, a particularly unexpected and pat one, that made it irre-
sistible. He talked always slowly, savoring his matter in a way
that took for granted and therefore challenged minute attention.

He was an incomparable mimic. He could look drunk entirely by
facial expression, with no easy staggering to help out. Then he
would become a Fourth of July orator, one hand between buttons of coat, the other with finger tips on table, head thrown
high, stilted voice beginning "Fellow Citizens." . . .

Ridgely had in his letters more than any other I have known the
Stevensonian faculty of pure, divine nonsense.[25]

It is clear that Torrence had finally found a real home at the Judson with a group of people who provided a strong impetus for his
work.

III   *Renewed Success*—Abelard *and* Heloise

In February, 1907, Scribner's published Torrence's verse drama,
Abelard and Heloise. While not as handsomely bound as his two
earlier books, it was an attractive little volume, and its critical
reception was even more favorable than that for *El Dorado.*
Torrence's former employer, Jeannette L. Gilder, wrote in the Chicago *Tribune* that "the poem deserves more than passing notice.
The fact that it is the first poetic treatment of one of the greatest
love stories in the world makes it conspicuous, and the fact that it
is treated by a young American poet and treated so well makes it
doubly important." [26] Miss Gilder's long review was far from being
the most enthusiastic, for *The Book Buyer's* critic proclaimed that
"Mr. Torrence has carried it off triumphantly. Its scalp, as it were,
dangles gracefully at his belt. In the first place he's made a play
of it—the play's truly the thing. . . . The diction is that to be
expected of the maturity of a poet in whose early work critics of
authority found unmistakeably the Promethean spark." [27]

Perhaps the highest praise was given by W. S. Braithwaite in
the Boston *Evening Transcript:* "Here is a new Romeo and Juliet

shorn of all physical tragedy and imbued with spiritual tragedy, nobler and more appealing. For its characterization, its marvelous poetry, its imagination and action, Mr. Torrence's *Abelard and Heloise* is a valuable and distinctive contribution to the American poetic drama, too poor in its possessions not to be loudly joyful with this rich gift." [28]

Abelard and Heloise is the re-creation of the medieval romance about the love of Abelard, a lecturer-priest and Master of the School of Notre Dame, for Heloise, the niece of the canon of Notre Dame. Abelard is torn between his love for Heloise and his devotion to his vocation which requires that he remain celibate. Because of the nature of Abelard's dilemma, the basic conflict is between worldly love and otherworldly devotion. Of course, love is the more powerful force, and when we first meet Abelard he is willing to renounce all for love: "I have cast off that world for great Love's sake/And have relinquished all my mighty dreams." [29] The power of the austere medieval church is not, however, easily thrown aside by Abelard; and the fanatical priest, Malart, devotes all of his energy to seeing that the love of Abelard and Heloise is destroyed and that both are punished. When Abelard is left a fortune and a title, Heloise's guardian gives his consent to her marriage, but Heloise, because of her devotion to Abelard and her respect for his vocation, refuses to marry him:

> He has been free before and shall be ever.
> Free to pursue the upward path he walks
> Toward that high radiance that is his ambition. (115)

Abelard does not understand Heloise's sacrifice, and when she begs for the continuance of his love, he misinterprets her action and thinks her wicked. Under the influence of Malart, Abelard takes his priestly vows and thus separates himself from Heloise forever:

> *Heloise:* I could take pleasure even from this thing
> But that you suffered. So there's nothing saved.
> *Abelard:* Silence is never lost, nor timeless peace.
> The courts of heaven are all white and still.
> Peace is best, for that I'll set my sail.
> A little longer your unquiet soul
> Will swim through its rough dreams, until at last

> It beaches on the dawn and finds its path;
> Meet me where peace is.
> (172–73)

The last act takes place twenty years after their romance. Heloise, who has become the beloved nurse of the young King Louis VII, is traveling with her master in a wood near the monastery in which Abelard is dying; and, in a neighboring valley, the young priest Astrolabus is urging the people to begin another Crusade. By a strange coincidence, the evil Malart is living as a hermit in a nearby cave, still anxious to bring vengeance upon the former lovers for their defiance of God's law. Astrolabus is the illegitimate son of Abelard and Heloise, and Malart cruelly exposes his scandalous birth in front of the young man's followers. After Abelard's final meeting with Heloise, Astrolabus, exposed and dishonored, enters and confronts his mother:

> Ah, you—you—I have often seen your face
> But now I know you, what you are to me.
> Well shameless cause, look on your shame's effect,
> For I am outcast, bloody, spit upon.
> I know your story out of common ballads.
> Why? Why? Say in what way had I unborn
> Ever done injury to you or wronged you
> That you should body forth my soul in shame.
> (212–13)

After cursing his mother, Astrolabus leaves. Abelard has just received notice of his excommunication—also the work of Malart—and dies from the shock, leaving Heloise alone on the stage for a final monologue:

> This is not twilight now.
> You are about me brightly in the air.
> Shine, then, upon this altar while I lay
> New vows upon it of more service to you.
> *She looks up.*
> For I'll live on and seek him out and win him
> Before I'll follow you to other fields.
> So hear me where you now are and be strong.
> Keep up the battle till I come to you,

And watch, protect, and shield him.
> *She turns her gaze upon Abelard's rigid form.*
Abelard!
> (p. 215)

Certainly *Abelard and Heloise* is a better structured drama than *El Dorado*. The settings are practical, and the action is far more economical than the earlier play; but, like Miss Peabody's attempts at poetic drama, *Abelard and Heloise* is too studied—too much an attempt at re-creating a lost genre. The scenes between the lovers are quite beautiful both as poetry and as dramatic representation, but the scenes with the secondary characters are gratuitous and overly long. The play would have been much improved if Torrence had been more economical and less anxious to create a work on a grand scale.

The language, too, is often overly inflated, and it is always far from the American idiom. There are eloquent moments, but there are also embarrassing ones:

> This very ground opposes coming day.
> The legions of the dew array their spears
> To fight until the upward-marching sun
> Dispels their watery camp.
> (56)

In short, *Abelard and Heloise*, like *El Dorado*, is the work of an artist striving for mastery in a form that was not congenial to him. He and his colleagues were conscientious in their efforts to create an American poetic drama, but their efforts were doomed from the start. The form, as they understood it, was alien to the American experience and to the American language, and the time had come to bridge the gap between American expression and American life. Surprisingly it was Edmund Clarence Stedman who gave the most cogent analysis of their failure:

> In short, I have been recently impressed by two things: first, the fulfillment of my long ago prediction of the dramatic quality which must attach to any renaissance of poetry. "Wisdom is justified of her children," and you form a school which I have looked for. But second . . . you will not have done your work at all until you show some evidence in it of the spirit of the New World.

. . . You only show your own limitations when you profess to show yourselves unable to find American atmosphere and themes for American dramas.[30]

Torrence, like Moody, was to find American themes for his plays; but the two men's ideal of poetic drama would have to be sacrificed. For Torrence as for Moody, the sacrifice proved beneficial.

CHAPTER 4

William Vaughn Moody and the
Prose Dramas

> Torrence and Robinson have the dra-
> matic fever acutely. Torrence has just
> finished a three acter which he is to
> read to me tonight. . . . Robinson
> thinks the play is a big thing.
> —William Vaughn Moody
> to Harriet Brainerd [1]

I *Moody and* The Madstone

IT is impossible to progress with this account of Torrence's career without pausing to discuss William Vaughn Moody, the
leader of the poetic circle of which Torrence was a devoted member. Few men have commended the reverence and devotion of
their comrades that Moody earned during his brief lifetime. In
him, other members of the Judson circle saw the embodiment of
all their poetic aspirations. He believed in the creation of an
American poetic tradition and in the revival of the poetic drama;
but, most important, he was successful, which was the best encouragement his colleagues could have. While some of Moody's
smaller poems such as "Gloucester Moors" and "Ode in Time of
Hesitation" are still anthology pieces, his important work for our
purposes is his poetic and prose drama. Moody's design was to
write a poetic trilogy on man's relation to God. The third part,
The Death of Eve, was never finished; but we do have *The
Masque of Judgment* and *The Fire Bringer. The Masque,* dealing
with God's judgment of man, is not a vindication of God's justice,
but a rather skeptical investigation of it. After two acts devoted to
the Incarnation and the crucifixion, the central portion of the play

deals with the day of judgment, which is pictured as a betrayal of man's promise of freedom by his creator, a betrayal that will lead to the downfall of God. *The Masque of Judgment* is also a defense, indeed a glorification, of man's passions—of the creative force within him that separates him from the animals.

The drama which Moody completed next, *The Fire Bringer,* is actually the first part of the trilogy; and it was written to be performed but, like most of the poetic plays of the period, was fated to become a closet drama. *The Fire Bringer* is a reworking of the Prometheus legend, but, unlike either Shelley or Aeschylus, Moody ends his story with the intimation of Zeus's punishment and devotes the drama to the events preceding it. Moody has made other major changes in the myth, for his Prometheus merely restores fire to man who had possessed it before the flood. What is most interesting to us is the Dionysian spirit of the drama—its praise of the passions and its unrestrained glorification of the spirit of man.

The final work of the trilogy, *The Death of Eve,* was intended to depict man's search for a reconciliation with God through Eve, the original cause of man's separation from his Creator. If anything stands at the center of this trilogy, it is love for man and his freedom, not in a political but in a spiritual sense. In order to be free, man had to defy his Creator who was imposing limits on his will. God retaliated; but, in destroying the creative power in man, he destroyed part of Himself. Finally, through Eve, man's creative force is united with that of God. William Norton Payne's assessment of the trilogy in *The Dial* is typical of the praise heaped upon Moody's work in the early part of the century: "The stupendous task which Moody set himself in the trilogy is the highest which poetry has ever attempted. It is the task of Aeschylus and Dante and Milton, the task of Goethe in his *Faust* and Shelley in his *Prometheus Unbound.* It is Milton's attempt to justify the ways of God to man coupled with the attempts of later poets to justify the ways of man to God." [2]

There is no doubt that Moody's interest in and success with the poetic drama was an inspiration to Torrence and was probably one of the factors influencing his sudden spurt of creative energy on *Abelard and Heloise* three years after he began it. By the time *Abelard* had been finished, however, Moody had successfully conquered a new area—the prose drama; and Torrence was not to be left behind. In 1906, Moody finished a prose drama entitled *The Sabine Woman*, which was inspired by a trip to the West, a trip which greatly impressed Moody and led him to see the West as a land where the human spirit could run free, unfettered by the harsh restrictions that had been placed on man in the East by his Puritan heritage. The play, although written in prose, is highly poetic, with a use of language and symbol that only a poet could manage.

The history of *The Sabine Woman* is one of those success stories that seem more fiction than truth. As Moody told a reporter after the play's immensely successful New York opening,

> I did not expect that it would attract any particular attention. In fact, I never dreamed that it would be produced. I wrote it because I wanted to write it, not with any hope that it would ever see the light. Its production was an accident. It had been finished for some time when I sent it to a friend in Chicago, an actor who knew Miss (Margaret) Anglin. She was playing there at the time, and one night, when she couldn't sleep, as she afterwards told me, she turned to a pile of plays that she kept in a table beside her bed. My play happened to be on top—that was an accident. She had intended reading only a few pages in the hope of inducing sleep, but the play kept her awake until she had finished it. The next day, Friday, she gave it to her manager to read, and on Saturday she put the play into rehearsal.[3]

The Chicago opening of *The Sabine Woman* was on April 12, 1906, and it played to large audiences throughout its run there. That summer Moody revised the play, changing its name to *The Great Divide*, and emphasizing its thematic ramifications. The finished work opened in New York at the Princess Theatre on October 3, 1906, in a production directed by Henry Miller who also played Ghent, and featuring Miss Anglin as Ruth. The critical reception and audience reaction were nothing short of fantastic for the time, and the play became a long-run success in both New York and London.

The Great Divide could not but have had an immense effect on Torrence. Its conflict between the wild Ghent, unfettered by the stifling effects of the Puritan ethic and as free as the country he roams, and Ruth, imprisoned by her New England conscience, was one with which Torrence could sympathize. After all, this conflict was closely akin to that between free love and the restrictions of a cold, unworldly morality that Torrence had created in *Abelard and Heloise.* Moreover, it was a truly American drama, not only in setting, but also in theme and expression. Moody had finally created what America had sorely lacked up to this time—a great American play—and Torrence was more than eager to follow in his footsteps. Just ten days after the opening in New York of *The Great Divide,* which Torrence and his friends attended, the Ohio poet wrote this letter to his parents: "I got the idea for a new play last night after I went to bed. It is modern and to be written in prose. It is to be called *The Madstone* and the scene laid in Ohio is just such a town as Xenia." [4]

For some reason, Torrence did not begin writing the play until Christmas Day, 1906, but the next month, his parents received news of its completion: "I first set pen to paper on it on Christmas Day so I will have been just eighteen days doing it, besides doing my regular work at the office. I was four years on *Abelard.* That shows how long it took me to learn the business. . . . I will begin another Xenia play week after next which Moody says will be even better than this." [5]

If Torrence could no longer draw on historical or mythical characters, he did have a new source for both character and myth: the very culture he had tried to rebel against—the world of Greene County, Ohio. Not only is the idea for *The Madstone* taken from local folklore and the setting in Greene County but the characters are also based on local figures: "I've got Tillie in the play and call her by name. The heroine's name is Lestra. The hero has had Frank Mower's record as a U. S. Consul." [6] This use of local figures caused his family some consternation; they feared that their son might anger some important Xenia people. Torrence, of course, allayed their fears: "Don't worry about me putting in McDowells or any one else. I haven't the remotest suggestion of the McDowells or anyone else so that it would be recognized in the slightest way." [7]

Unlike Moody, Torrence created his play with the intention of having it produced as soon and as successfully as possible. Of course, Moody was the man to help Torrence gain a producer for his play, and Torrence read it to him the evening it was completed. Moody, impressed by his friend's new play, took it to actor-producer Henry Miller with the hope that Miller would show it to his client, the Russian actress Alla Nazimova. Torrence shrewdly had dedicated *Abelard and Heloise* to Mme Nazimova with the hope that such an honor would put him in her favor. The fondest wish of any young playwright of the time would be to have his play produced by Miller with Nazimova in the leading role, for their names on the marquee guaranteed recognition.

Two weeks after Torrence had read his play to Moody, he was invited to read it to Henry Miller, who was impressed enough to pass the manuscript on to the great Nazimova. Torrence's account of her reaction to his play bears an uncanny resemblance to Moody's account of Margaret Anglin's first reading of *The Sabine Woman:*

> You know by the telegram that the play is accepted. Mme. Nazimova is most enthusiastic about it. It will not be produced until autumn because it is too late this season to put on a great play. I wonder if you realize what this means; to have her take the play. It means that I have written and will continue to write for one of the three greatest actresses in the world for one thing. The Miller management and Madame have been struggling through piles of mss. plays and they had not found one that touched her. This became known and, as Robinson says, the whole country was writing for her. Miller gave her my play Tuesday night and when she went to her rooms at one o'clock at night she was tired and Miller hadn't said anything to her about the play but just handed it to her and said here's another play. As I say, she reached home very tired and was going to bed when she picked up the play and began turning the pages carelessly, thinking another one of those plays. All at once she began to read and read through the first act and looked up at the clock and it was two o'clock. She then read the rest of it and didn't go to bed until five o'clock in the morning although she had two performances the next day. She was wild with delight. She raised her hand and said, "I swear to you that I will play that play" and gave me her hand on it. "Why," said she, "do you think I'd let that play get by me?" [8]

While *The Madstone* might seem rickety to modern sensibilities, it was a sincere attempt to duplicate the success, both artistically and commercially, of *The Great Divide*. Like Torrence's mentor, Torrence uses a controlling image to give the play its basic unity: the madstone, an irregular shaped stone that was supposed to have the power of healing infections. As Nick Chase, the owner of one of these stones says, "I've seen a madstone applied to an infected wound until it had filled itself with the virus. Then it dropped off." [9] The box which contains Nick's madstone has the following inscription: "By this stone and in the name of love I draw out poison." Of course, nearly everyone in the play wants to use the stone: Mrs. North wants to keep it in her clock for good luck; Turtle Dan, to cure his drunkenness; and Bess Worden, to cure her son's serious infection. The madstone also is a symbol for the play's heroine. Lestra Doane; for she, newly married, is most unhappy. She feels that she can no longer love, and she does not understand why; but neither, of course, does her husband Edwin, who tries to regain her affection:

Doane: You have raised me up to you. You have purified me.
Lestra: Whatever you say, don't say that again—never, never.
Doane: What?
Lestra: That I have purified you.
Doane: Why not? It's true.
Lestra: I don't know. Somehow that has something to do with what's wrong. It maddens me beyond words to hear it.

As the play progresses, Lestra recognizes the symbolic value of the madstone and of her relationship to it—a relationship she shares with all women:

For we're madstones, madstones that draw out the poison with which life has envenomed us. . . . You select those of us who are perfectly innocent of your experience. Ah, yes, you love our innocence. You want a perfectly spotless surface which you can tint all over again with the hues of your personality. You are all artists, I think. You apply a tint here, a little red there, a poisonous green within, hints of forbidden things, suggestions half caught and in the name of love we cling to you until we ourselves have it all here, here (*striking her breast*) where we can never get rid of it,—we know all that you know and we imagine far more. Our minds are filled with poison until we can hold no more. And then—Do you know what the madstone does when it has served its purpose?
                    (*Doane gazes at her speechlessly*)
I think I'll have to tell you. When the madstone has all the poison it can hold—it drops off.

During the course of the play, Lestra realizes that she can still love, through her love for her former childhood companion, Nick Chase: "I inspired a real love, a true love, a love that could give me up because it loved me. I knew that another man really needed me and that I had not lost my blessing of healing." Despite her love for Chase, Lestra turns from both men at the end of the play—a sign of Torrence's reluctance to condone adultery publicly and to leave Lestra with an unhappy marriage.

There is little in *The Madstone* that is of literary interest, but it is easy to see how, in the age of David Belasco, a serious actress could be enthusiastic about the possibility of playing the leading role. Lestra offered Nazimova just the sort of intense, brooding personality she liked to portray. This suitability was no coincidence; for, from the very beginning of his interest in playwrighting, Torrence was careful to tailor his plays to the talents of particular performers: "I write each play having in mind a particular well known actor or actress and then try to make the central part one which will just suit them." [10] The evidence suggests that *The Madstone* was written with Nazimova clearly in mind.

II *Europe and Disillusionment*

Despite Torrence's pleasure about the acceptance of *The Madstone*, the first months of 1907 were not happy ones for him. The combination of the routine of his work at *Cosmopolitan* and of his feverish artistic activity weakened his constitution and once again threatened to disable him. Noticing Torrence's ill health and his crucial need for a change in climate, the Ledoux family offered him a sizable "loan" to take a European tour. As soon as the offer was made, Torrence asked Moody to be his traveling companion, an offer Moody found most congenial. Torrence, feeling the blush of success over the signing of the contract for *The Madstone*, quit his job, took a short trip to Xenia, and returned to sail with Moody on March 9, 1917. The itinerary was an exciting one:

We disembarked at Gibraltar and a day or two later put to sea again in a small coasting boat from which we landed at Tangier. During our stay there we were turned back from a projected journey to Fez by the activities of a moorish bandit Rasuli who made it his business to capture Americans for ransom. Tangier at that time had just been occupied by the French but was completely untouched by any visible European influence affecting its manners or customs. Its atmosphere was that of the Arabian Nights. For example though the slave markets were no longer open they existed under cover and we were constantly solicited to load ourselves up with human chattels. From Tangier we sailed up the coast and entered Spain by landing at Cadiz. From there we went to Seville and were there during Holy Week, a pageant which for us was compounded of religious processions and bull fighting. From Seville we went to Granada where we stayed at a little hotel on the Alhambra hill, spending our time between the palace and gardens there and the gipsies who lived in caves on the hills beyond. After this we went north to Madrid, spending most of our days at the Prado among the Velasquez's and the Goya's. From Madrid we went to Toledo principally to see the El Greco's. On our return south we stopped at Cordova and then went on to Gibraltar where we set sail for Naples. During our stay at Naples we made journeys to Pompeii and to Paistum to see the splendid Greek temples, better survived than any. From Naples we went on to Rome, to Florence, to Venice where during our stay we debated whether we should go around the world. From Venice we went to Lucerne, from there to Paris, and later to England.[11]

Moody's letters to Harriet Brainerd display nothing but enthusiasm about the travels of the two writers and about the company of his traveling companion: "Ridgely proves to be a capital travelling companion, self supporting, good humored, and sensitive to all the varied excitements, small and large, which make up the poet of travel. His health is good, and there seems to be no danger that there is anything radically the matter with him."[12] However, Torrence, despite his feeling that "Will is a perfectly splendid traveling companion," was not altogether happy during his European sojourn. He wrote his parents the following dejected letter on April 16:

I haven't much to say about my travels. I haven't gotten nearly as much out of them so far as I expected. I had grown stale in my enthusiasm about Europe. I had seen it too late. I should have gone when I was twenty one and continued to come throughout my twenties as Moody did. I have gotten too old. It is a great disappointment to me so far. I can see constantly how it would have benefitted me earlier but it is too late now.

. . . I was pretty sure that I was losing a great deal by not getting to see it then but I still hoped that it would keep. But it
hasn't. It is merely picturesque to me now. Merely a luxury. It
was a necessity once.[13]

Not all was happiness for Moody either, for Torrence wrote his
parents early in May that Moody "is having more trouble with his
leg. He had a tumour removed from just above his knee a year
and a half ago and since coming over here it has begun to grow
again which proves it malignant." [14] Because of this problem, the
pair sailed from England on May 29 for their native shores.

III   The Thunder Pool

If Europe did not excite Torrence, as he had hoped it would, it
did rest and strengthen him for a flurry of creative activity. He
returned to New York jobless but undaunted. With financial support from his more successful friends, especially Moody, he worked
on his wedding and funeral rituals—nonsectarian replacements
for the church liturgy. In July, he returned to Xenia where he
worked on a new play, *The Thunder Pool*. When he returned to
New York in October, he found to his dismay that Mme Nazimova had lost interest in appearing in *The Madstone;* but Henry
Miller still showed an interest in the play and offered Torrence a
guarantee of $1,750 if the play was not produced. Finally, Miller
admitted to Torrence that he could not risk a production of *The
Madstone* without a strong female star, nor did he show interest
in *The Thunder Pool*.

Like its predecessor, *The Thunder Pool* was an attempt to emu-
late Ibsen and integrate poetic symbolism and dramatic realism.
It, too, is constructed around a central symbol from the folklore of
Ohio. The thunder pool was a mythical deep pool that absorbed
all the energy of the lightning that was attracted to it: "All the
lightning that no mortal eye sees sinks with its stabbing weight
into the still thunder pool until at last the pool is seething with the
fire and storm of it through all its depths." [15] The heroine, Lois, is,
of course the embodiment of the myth of the thunder pool as
Lestra Doane was of the madstone. Like Lestra, Lois is moody
and withdrawn—something of a female Byronic hero—who qui-
etly resists the pressures of her society. Finally, through her love

for John Edgewood, a temperamental young man fleeing from a lynch gang that will hang him for a murder he did not commit, she is freed from the turbulence within her. After spending the night with him while she hides him in her studio, she defends her actions to her father in this way:

> I am innocent even in the world's sense. I am only guilty of being found and being set free. For the first time in my life I felt free and I acted as my nature led me to do. My lover came and kissed me and led me out into the storm. I was obliged to protect his life and I led him to my own place to shelter him. All is well now. You have wanted me to be happy. It was not for you or me to choose the path by which my happiness came. I love him. He is my mate. You see, I was a prisoner so long, everything had grown so still outside me, and when the storm came it was very terrible and swift.

Of course, Lois's father just happens to be a justice of the peace, so the conflict with the moral code is very neatly taken care of by a quick marriage; and everyone lives happily ever after. It is interesting to note the thematic elements shared by *The Madstone* and *The Thunder Pool:* both are dominated by a strong female who is at odds with established morality but who eventually falls under its dictates rather than openly rebel against it. Lestra leaves both men rather than violate her wedding vows by giving herself to the man she really loves; and, despite the fact that Lois has spent the night with her lover, she declares herself pure and is immediately and happily married to him. It seems that, despite his disdain for the stern moral code of his parents, Torrence could not bring himself to advocate violation of it in his plays. Also of interest is his attempt at development of the dramatic symbol. Unlike Moody, however, Torrence found it necessary to spell it out—to make sure that his audience apprehended the connection between the symbol and the action of the play. Needless to say, this tendency emerges as a weakness rather than as a strength. There is no need for Moody to explain the title of *The Great Divide,* for the action of the play does that effectively without such explicit reference. Perhaps, as in Torrence's poetry, he was to find that he was more effective when he worked on a smaller scale.

During the next few years, Torrence maintained the pace he had set for himself during 1907. He wrote his parents in January,

1908: "I am working as never before. I am doing poems at a perfectly tremendous rate, a whole poem a day! I have done a complete one already today and shall now work at a new one this afternoon. I expect to get out a volume of poems. I never felt so much like work before nor did it flow so freely." [16] Despite this poetic inspiration, Torrence had no intention of giving up his attempts at achieving success as a playwright; for he wrote his parents in March, 1908: "I am going to write for the stage as a profession and by God's help I expect to keep at it steadily until I win out. There is nothing like never saying die." [17]

Torrence was not the only one of his circle still devoted to playwrighting. Despite his failing health, Moody was working as hard as he could on The Faith Healer; and Robinson was making a feverish attempt at becoming a dramatist. During the summer of 1908, Torrence wrote Moody the following comment about Robinson: "I found E. A. R. drilling away in the tower of the Judson. He has finished his third three act play, which with the two curtain raisers makes five in all and he is setting about another to be done before the end of summer. He is miserable of course, because he is happy, but fortunately he is happy because he is miserable." [18] Torrence seemed a bit envious of Robinson's job in the New York Customs House—a job given to him by President Theodore Roosevelt, who was an admirer of his poetry:

> Robinson will soon get a raise in position and salary in the Customs service. He is certainly very lucky as he does no work whatever. He is frightfully lazy, sleeps until noon and sometimes until four o'clock in the afternoon and complains when he has to go down to the office to draw up his pay twice a month. But Roosevelt stands behind him and sees to it that he keeps his job although they have lately fired many hard working employees from his office. He gets on my nerves sometimes with his lamentations over salary day breaking into his rest. He isn't doing much writing even.[19]

Moreover, Torrence often became justly impatient with Robinson's excessive drinking. He related one encounter with Robinson in another letter to Moody: "I found E. A. R. in that hell hole of a Guffanti's last night deep in his soup. I seized him, rubbed him down with an onion so that I would recognize him again and then buried the onion. He said I was a fishmonger. I'll speak to him again." [20]

If Torrence found Robinson's financial security enviable, he must have found Moody's doubly so; for the success of *The Great Divide* had left Moody more than secure. Moody's affluence was advantageous, however, to the impoverished Ohio poet who was not reluctant to acknowledge his generosity: "You're the best that ever was and is and as good as any that shall be. The double power check came this morning, yellow with youth, hope, and the dayspring. It makes me ache a little for near as you are to me I hate to confess myself even to you so limp. But evidently time and the devil and the flies conspire somehow to keep us from feeling too damned continuously independent." [21]

IV *The Rituals*

While Torrence's output was not so prodigious as his claims lead one to think, his published poems during the next few years, though few, are worthy of close reading. His major project, which finally reached publication in *Century Magazine* in August and September, 1909, was the composition of the "Rituals for Birth and Naming," "The Ritual for Marriage," and "The Ritual for the Body's Passing." The last-named, although written first, was not published until the *Hesperides* volume of 1925. Torrence's initial comment on "The Ritual for the Body's Passing" is illuminating: "The Funeral Ritual is full of hope and faith, in fact that is the whole purpose of it, to give people a rational ground for faith, something that their reasonable minds can get hold of." [22]

Torrence's correspondence since his arrival in New York attests to his disillusionment with the faith of his fathers. As early as 1901, Torrence had written his parents that "There is not one phase of denominational Christianity that I don't loathe from the bottom of my soul; cold, sordid, ignorant, hypocritical as it is. The longer I live the more I hate it. I remember when I was sick last winter and thought I was going to die, I thought if I could get well long enough to publically sever my connection with a thing that offered so little spiritual solace, I would die easier." [23] If Torrence found the church loathsome, "Rituals" attest to his need for some sort of religious belief. It is interesting to note, too, that the Rituals, with their insistence on the world of the spirit, were written at the time that Torrence's friend William Vaughn Moody was putting the finishing touches on *The Faith Healer*, his dramatic affirmation of the world of the spirit.

Torrence's *Ritual for the Body's Passing* asserts the cyclic nature of life—

> To the glowing feast of birth
> All the distant guests return;
> Nothing pauses in the earth.[24]

—and the eternal world of the spirit. The poem ends with the sea, one of Torrence's favorite images for the source and continuity of life:

> Not from the shore may any requiem swell
> Nor winging of farewell
> From us within the bubble Time or Place;
> We are already on the water's face,
> And wave with wave shall endlessly ally,
> Too near for need of summons to recall.
> The end of earth is the beginning sky;
> The sea is under all,
> From whose unfathomed wells we rise and flow
> Slowly along a winding glory, seeing
> The wise unrest from which we had our being
> And the ineffable to which we go.[24]

In the "Ritual for Birth and Naming," we see that Torrence has replaced the traditional concept of the soul with that of the spirit, chained for a brief time to the body, but soon to be free once more. The child is named, "In the three names of Love, Light, and Divine Humanity." [25]

Torrence finally found a religion he could wholeheartedly embrace in Thomas Troward's Mental Science, a movement whose central belief was that man could come into a strengthening contact with the universal life force through the careful control of the subjective mind. Not only is one able to meet life's problems more successfully, but one also can heal physical ills since they are really products of wrong beliefs about one's self. A letter to his brother in 1911 shows Troward's effect on Torrence:

> We are on the eve of a great age of the world a great new spiritual awakening. The church as it stands today is dead and full of dry bones. But the spiritual needs of men have resulted in the rising of a fresh wave from the true waters, and when I say "spiritual needs" I don't mean any far away cant such as we have in the churches. I mean the kind of thing you yourself revealed in your last letter to me when you said something about making one more try of it as a writer before you confessed yourself a failure. Well you were then unconsciously giving a hint of a spiritual need. You had begun to suspect your ability. But mark my words and then think; The Spirit of Life never *wants* to waste. Everything you ever imagined you *might* do *It* will help you to fully accomplish if you will turn to it intelligently and allow It to do it. And to learn to do this intelligently I think you might read this Troward book [*Edinburgh Lectures on Mental Science*] to begin with. . . . It is the perfect way; to yield yourself to the spirit of the age in which you are fortunate enough to be born.[26]

While there is little doubt that the ugly face of fact modified the extremity of Torrence's faith, he never totally gave up his belief in a sort of neo-Platonic spirit world of which the material world was something of a faulty replica, nor did he ever renounce his belief in the power of the spirit over the flesh.

Torrence's mysticism seems to have found its most substantial form in the "Rituals," which were written before he gave his beliefs the more definite form of Troward's Mental Science. His other poems of this period are not as metaphysically oriented, but they do show Torrence at the top of his form. "Three O'Clock," which was first published in *Scribner's Magazine* in December, 1908, is an example of such a work and stands as one of Torrence's finest pieces:

> The jewel-blue electric flowers
> Are cold upon their trees,
> Upraised, the deadly harp of rails
> Whines for its interval of ease.
> The stones kept all their daily speech

Buried, but can no more forget
Than could a water-vacant bench
The hour when it was wet.

A whitened few wane out like moons,
Ghastly from some torn edge of shade;
A drowning one, a reeling one,
And one still loitering after trade.
On high the candor of a clock
Portions the dark with solemn sound.
The burden of the bitten rock
Moans up from underground.

Far down the street a shutting door
Echoes the yesterday that fled
Among the days that should have been
Which people cities of the dead.
The banners of the steam unfold
Upon the towers to meet the day;
The lights go out in red and gold,
But time goes out in gray.[27]

The simplicity and the economy of this poem ally it much
more closely to the future than to the past. We see in the poem
Torrence's usual interest in color imagery and in metaphorical
language, but most effective are the many metaphors which are
all apt and all combine to project a sense of desolation. Often, as
in the initial "jewel-blue electric flowers," the metaphors have an
ironic connotation, suggesting the loss of the natural world in the
wake of the cities. There are moments when the language veers
toward Victorian poetic diction ("the banners of the steam"), but
the overall effect remains impressive. "Three O'Clock" is Torrence's first "modern" poem, and its vivid picture of the desolation
of a city at night looks ahead to T. S. Eliot's "Rhapsody on a
Windy Night."

The longing to create a successful play still haunted Torrence,
for he wrote Moody in 1907: "I have been here in Xenia nearly all
summer. I go as much as possible among the darkies and country
people and have picked up some folklore material. It is mostly
useful—what I've found lately—for comedy and I believe it would
make a cow laugh." [28] He wrote another regional play, _Any-_

one With Half An Eye, which never got beyond the manuscript stage; but he continued to be sensitive to new ideas for his plays.

On October 17, 1910, a disaster struck that left an indelible mark on Torrence. After a long illness William Vaughn Moody died of a brain tumor at the tragically young age of forty-one and, so it seems, at the apex of his creativity. A letter to Daniel Gregory Mason, dated October 22, 1910, is a most eloquent statement of Torrence's reaction to the death of his friend and inspiration:

Last night at midnight when I returned from Chicago I found a letter from Miss Dunbar in which she said that you had heard nothing about his latter days and the change. Somehow I have felt and I still feel that you were dearer to him than any man besides Stickney and so it is like coming nearer to him to speak to you. Last Saturday—a week ago this afternoon he was able to take a short walk across a park beside his cottage. He walked perhaps a hundred yards and played with his dog. By "playing" I mean that he laughed cheerfully at its antics. He was comparatively free from pain. Upon returning he felt very weak and was persuaded to lie down. He seemed however, to be fairly easy after dinner and retired with no expression of feeling differently. About midnight he was seized with unusual pain which increased until Sunday afternoon at five o'clock when he became unconscious and so continued until two o'clock on Monday morning when he left us. A healer was with them and Charlotte cried upon him to bring Will back from the dead. . . . I stayed in his room. He had your picture on his mantel shelf. There was none like him, none. I for one shall never fear again to die since he has gone ahead on that path. I looked upon his face before they gave his body to fire. He had departed at the last in peace I think. I am not sorry I went there. I feel that I received a benediction. Mrs. Moody left me alone with his body for half an hour. I wished only for you then, he seemed to be about me and make me think of you. . . . I feel that he is constantly shedding his spirit upon mine since he became invisible. I feel conscious of him in every good thing. . . . Surely he was and is one of the mightiest of the sons of God and we were blessed beyond most mortals in being his lovers. And I feel that he will not forget us who loved him with all our hearts but that he will leave signs and messages for us as he journeys from star to star, so that we may find him when we follow by that way. . . . Yet his most fine gold shall never become dim nor his sacred ashes scattered

in vain for he told us eternally of eternal things. . . . The things
of this world can never again appear the same to me after this
and I thank God for that at least.[29]

Torrence was with Harriet and Charlotte Moody and Ferdinand
Schevill on that brisk October 28 when Moody's ashes were scattered to the sea from the beach at Far Rockaway after the four
had read together Moody's *The Fire Bringer*. After the ashes were
scattered, they knelt and Harriet recited the Ninety-first Psalm.

As a tribute to Moody, his dear friend and mentor, perhaps it is
not too melodramatic to say his idol, Torrence wrote "Santa Barbara Beach," a memorial to Moody's last home. Though Torrence
had never seen this scenic California town, he certainly felt in-
tensely its meaning for Moody—and for him.

> Now while the sunset offers,
> Shall we not take our own;
> The gems, the blazing coffers,
> The seas, the shores, the throne?
>
> The sky-ships, radiant masted
> Move out, bear low our way.
> Oh, Life was dark while it lasted,
> Now for enduring day.
>
> Now with the world far under,
> To draw up drowning men
> And show them lands of wonder
> Where they may build again.
>
> There earthly sorrow falters,
> There longing has its wage;
> There gleam the ivory altars
> Of our lost pilgrimage.
>
> —Swift flame—then shipwrecks only
> Beach in the ruined light;
> Above them reach up lonely
> The headlands of the night.
>
> A hurt bird cries and flutters
> Her dabbled breast of brown;

The western wall unshutters
To fling one last rose down.

A rose, a wild light after—
And life calls through the years,
"Who dreams my fountain's laughter
Shall feed my wells with tears." [30]

Here in these seven short stanzas is a hymnlike affirmation of
the immortality of the spirit. The central image of the poem is
that of the setting sun, that rose flung from the "western wall."
Torrence is using a common image here for the end of man's
earthly light, but he reverses the sense of the image in the second
stanza: "Oh, life was dark while it lasted,/Now for enduring day."
Above this world, above "the headlands of the night," is "our lost
pilgrimage," the world of the immortal spirit.

The concluding three stanzas provide a contrast to the exultant
tone of what has preceded. We are back on the desolate beach as
the last rays of the setting sun offer their "wild light." Instead of
the "sky ships radiant masted" bearing the death-liberated spirits,
we have only the hurt bird, a Whitmanesque symbol of earthly
longing and suffering. The longing that "feeds my wells with
tears" is not the longing for the return of the departed soul, but
the longing for the liberation of death. The style of the poem is
characteristic: simple stanzaic form and simple vocabulary as the
vehicle for a play of images.

"Santa Barbara Beach" was first published in one of the earliest
issues of *Poetry: A Magazine of Verse*, the journal so closely associated with "the new poetry." Perhaps a tribute to Moody in those
pages is a bit ironic, for he represented the type of poetry against
which the new poets rebelled, but it is significant that Torrence
was already casting his lot with the forces of the future in American poetry.

CHAPTER 5

The Negro Plays

> I have sometimes imagined that the Negro, other things being equal, might produce the greatest, the most direct, the most powerful drama in the world.[1]

THE five-year span preceding the premiere of Torrence's play *Granny Maumee* in 1914 was a time of inactivity for Torrence, and there are a number of possible explanations for his creative doldrums. Moody's death was undoubtedly one of the reasons for the silence, but it can hardly be considered the primary one. A more likely factor would be the disillusionment Torrence felt over his lack of success with his dramatic writing, for none of his prose plays had been produced or published. He was out of work and dependent financially upon the generosity of his family and friends. Any of these factors could have led to this period of disillusionment or depression which hampered his creativity.

Torrence still considered New York his home during these years, but he was forced to spend a good deal of time in Xenia where he was supported by his family. He also spent some time at a roominghouse in Cos Cob, Connecticut, where living was less costly than in the city. Records and correspondence from the years 1909–14 are scarce, and what does exist is of little importance to a study of Torrence's literary career.

I *Marriage*

The years from 1914 to 1917, however, were also crucial years for Torrence personally; moreover, they did more than any other period to establish his place in the inner circle of American literary figures. On the evening of February 3, 1914, Torrence's parents were awakened by the following telegram: "Was married this evening to Olivia Dunbar and stole march on Findley." [2] Torrence and Miss Dunbar had been friends since the young poet had moved into the Judson in 1906. In fact, he was infatuated with the young, attractive writer of short stories during the first months of their acquaintance, but their correspondence shows little mention of marriage. It seems possible that their decision to get married at this time was linked to Torrence's hopes for his new Negro plays. Jobless as he had been for so many years, he saw the plays as the new hope for a financial return from his work. Whatever their reasons for marriage after such a delay, time proved it to be a happy one. Of course, one of their well-wishers was their old friend from the Judson days, Edwin Arlington Robinson. Robinson's note seems strangely reserved, but it is not atypical of the poet:

> I have no means of knowing how much or how little my best wishes are worth to either of you, but you may be sure that you have them, and that they are entirely genuine. I was not very much surprised by the news, for the occurrence seemed in the order of things likely to happen.
>
> I hope most sincerely that all will go well with you, and that you will forgive me for not saying so in more brilliant language.[3]

Chard Powers Smith, in his recent biography of Robinson, reports that Torrence, not long before his death, had admitted that Robinson was in love with Olivia and was upset on returning from Peterborough, New Hampshire, in the fall of 1912 to find Olivia engaged to Torrence. Smith cites this incident as the cause for the "lapse in their (R.T. and E.A.R.) former intimacy" that followed.[4] This statement might be convincing were it not for Torrence's report next year (1915) that he and Olivia had been seeing "a good deal" of Robinson.[5]

II *The Significance of the Negro Plays*

Although Torrence's plays about Negroes did have great success at the box office, their place in the memory of this generation of theatergoers is virtually nonexistent. However, his three *Plays for a Negro Theatre* made a place for the Negro in serious

American dramatic literature. As Edith J. R. Isaacs notes in her study, *The Negro in the American Theatre*, "They marked . . . a turning point in Negro theatre history. They broke completely with all theatre stereotypes of Negro character. They gave Negro actors a first fine opportunity. They made Negroes welcome in the audience. They showed that Negroes could appreciate a white man's contribution to the literature of their life, if it were written in truth and beauty." [6] These plays, then, opened the door for the Negro in our theater.

Soon other serious playwrights, both white and Negro, turned to the Negro as a rich source of dramatic material. In the 1920's, Eugene O'Neill wrote *The Emperor Jones*, that brilliant study of man's descent from king to savage through fear and superstition. The 1930's brought Marc Connelly's delightful folk play, *Green Pastures;* DuBose Heyward's picture of life in Charleston's Catfish Row, *Porgy*, later to become Gershwin's great folk opera; and the federal theater's brilliant all-Negro *Macbeth.* More recently we have seen Langston Hughes, Lorraine Hansberry, Ossie Davis, and LeRoi Jones depict the Negro with an honesty that is at times delightful but often unsettling.

We have come to take the Negro's place on the American stage for granted; but, before Torrence's plays, the Negro and his problems were rarely presented on the legitimate stage in any form. Of course, *Uncle Tom's Cabin* had been a standby during the previous century, but it was popular when its antislavery theme was safely out of date. The only previous twentieth-century play to consider the Negro was Edward Sheldon's *The Nigger*, which had enjoyed a fair amount of success in the 1909–10 season. The play was not really about Negroes but about the crisis that occurs when the governor of a southern state is discovered to have some Negro blood. The problem is treated in a tabloid fashion that makes good theater, but it has little relation to real social concerns. The only Negro who appears is an old mammy, the sister of our hero's quadroon grandmother, and she emerges as nothing more than a stereotype of the faithful Negro servant. The play does not suggest that the hero should be accepted as he was before the discovery of his origins, despite his Negro blood. As a matter of fact, the hero himself rejects this idea: "Black's black, an' white's white. If yo' not one, yo' the othah, Geo'gie. I've always said that, an' I reckon I'll have to stick to't now!" [7]

If Torrence's plays did not explore the social problems of the Negro in America, such as poverty and inequality, in a way that would satisfy the Negro in our era of civil rights protests, they did for the first time present the Negroes as human beings with all the dignity and potential for both comedy and tragedy that they deserve. Moreover, their production was the first all-Negro performance of a serious play in the legitimate theater.

There seem to be two reasons for Torrence's new interest in Negro drama, both of which are presented in a statement he made in *Crisis* in 1917:

> I have sometimes imagined that the Negro, all other things being equal, might produce the greatest, the most direct, the most powerful drama in the world.
>
> And then, of course, it was not only the capacities of the Negro as actor that I wished to exploit in my plays. It was also the extraordinary dramatic richness of his daily life. . . . In modern life, the Negro comes face to face with many tragedies unknown to the Anglo-Saxon. And then, of course, his natural buoyancy of disposition produces a wealth of comedy which all the world has now learned to love. The parallel of all this with the Irish race and its national drama made a deep impression on me. I wanted to make the experiment, and try to contribute something, if I could, to a possible Negro drama, as vital and charming as the Irish.[8]

The first reason, then, is Torrence's enthusiasm for Irish folk drama, caused by the American visits of the Abbey Theatre. The Irish Players from the Abbey had made their first appearance in New York at the Maxine Elliott Theatre on Thirty-ninth Street on November 20, 1911. The repertoire included the greatest products of the Irish renaissance: Synge's *Riders to the Sea* and *The Playboy of the Western World*, Lady Gregory's *The Workhouse Ward*, Yeats's *Kathleen na Houlihan*, and Shaw's *The Shewing-Up of Blanco Posnet*. Because of the success of their engagement, the company returned the next season to present a repertory, beginning on February 4, 1913, at Wallack's Theatre. Torrence was strongly impressed by the folk drama the Irish had developed and saw great possibilities for such a form on the American stage.

We must remember, however, that the Irish players merely strengthened an interest in folk material that was already evident

in Torrence's earlier plays, *The Madstone* and *The Thunder Pool*.
In both those plays folk legends provided the central symbol. Yet
it had been six years since these plays were completed. In all
probability the impact of the Irish players was enough to counter-
act Torrence's disillusionment with the failure of his two prose
plays and to kindle his desires to create an American folk drama.

His new interest in the Negro as the source for his plays is not
difficult to explain. Before the Civil War, Torrence's home town of
Xenia, Ohio, was an important stop on the underground railroad,
the route by which runaway slaves escaped to Canada with the
aid of Northern Abolitionists. Because of this, and because of its
southwestern position in the state, not far from the Kentucky
border, many Negroes also came to Xenia to settle after the Civil
War. Near it, one of the country's major Negro colleges, Wilber-
force University, developed. Thus Negroes played an important
part in the life of Xenia, and in Torrence's childhood:

> When I was a boy, I saw a great deal of my colored townsmen
> who occupied Xenia's "East End." Xenia, by the way, is a concen-
> trated patch of Southern flavor and tradition, having been the
> focal point of immigration from all the Southern states for sixty
> years before the Civil War.
>
> I didn't deliberately seek the Negroes out. They were there and
> they were entertaining playmates. Their ways became as familiar
> to me as the ways of my own relatives. Their speech, their voices,
> their laughter, evoked an unconscious but perfectly sympathetic
> mimicry; so that Negro dialect became the only language not my
> own that I have ever learned to speak with facility and I believe
> with pretty complete accuracy.[9]

In his unpublished autobiography, Torrence tells of his later
contact with the Negroes of Xenia while working on his father's
farm during his periodic visits home during the early years of this
century:

> In October, as soon as the black frost came, it was time to have
> the pigs to market. This was always a little earlier by day and in
> the slow horse drawn trucks under the early afternoon sun, the
> pigs would "drift" and reduce their poundage by many degrees.
> But by night, usually under the moon, these treks were not only
> the wisest but also filled with romance. Usually the drivers con-
> sisted of my brother, four Negroes—Zachariah Letts, the tenant
> on our farm, a tall gaunt brown man unquestionably of Arab

descent; Milo Alexander, also an evident Arab or Moor, with a hawk nose and majestic curly beard; Cal Hatcher, foreman in our lumber yard, a mulatto; Alec Morgan, a powerful full blooded black elder—and myself. Behind us all, in the low phaeton, sat my father, driving our wise old mare, Gipsy, a household deity, proceeding at a snail's pace, always adapting her sensitive discernment to the situation. As we passed the various sleeping homesteads, the Negroes would converse with each other regarding their owners past and present.

"Das de old Conklin place. Man, many's de time I wuk in dem fields for ole man Conklin. Well, man, you never hear word from him no more."

"Well, you ain' goin' to wuk fer him no more."

"How come?"

"He done fell asleep in Jesus."

"Man, you're telling me somethin'. I ain' never hear dat. When was dis?"

"Way back yondah."

"Now look at his here place, beyont. Who live here now?"

"Man, dat's de sheepinest-raisin' man dat we ever had. But I thought dat was de ole Galloway place?"

"It uster be but Sheep Macmillan took it from de court."

"How come dat?"

"De farm finally come down to Bill Galloway an' you know about him?"

"Dat drinkin' man?"

"Drinkinest man I ever knew. Drink it all up." [10]

As with most of Torrence's experiences in his native region, it was quite a while before he decided to use his knowledge and memories of the Negroes of Xenia as the basis of a literary creation. Just as his poetry showed a greater freedom and mastery of his medium when he used familiar, regional material, his Negro plays, stemming as they did from his own experiences, displayed an economy and mastery of dramaturgy absent from his earlier poetic dramas. Moreover, just as his shorter lyric poems showed a decided improvement over his more ambitious pieces, the one-act Negro plays are much more successful than the early attempts at full-length dramas. Torrence had obviously discovered for himself that he was a miniaturist as well as a regionalist. Most important, however, was the fulfillment of the attempts made in the earlier prose plays to achieve poetic drama in prose as Moody had in *The Great Divide*.

III *The Production of the Negro Plays*

The late winter of 1914 brought with it the first stage presentation of one of Torrence's Negro plays, *Granny Maumee,* the first of his plays to be produced. In February, Torrence wrote Harriet Moody of the proposed production: "The pieces are both Negro plays. One I have now written within the past ten days and handed in yesterday. The other is already on the way. The producer is an organization called the Play Society. It pays no money and gives but two performances of each play but the productions are made to give plays a start and try to create a popular demand for popular performances. The Society is composed of practical professional people and the Frohmans furnish the Lyceum Theatre." [11]

The play was presented during the last week in March; and, in accordance with the policy of the Play Society, it was given a public matinee on Monday preceded by an invitational dress rehearsal the night before. As is usually the case with special Sunday performances, the audience for the unveiling of *Granny Maumee* was composed largely of theater people on a busman's holiday. *Granny Maumee* was preceded on the bill by a heavily cut revival of *A Woman Killed with Kindness,* Heywood's Jacobean potboiler, which was probably intended to be the chef d'œuvre. Typical of the enthusiastic critical reception of *Granny Maumee* was the review by Carl Van Vechten in the New York *Press:*

> There has been no more important contribution made to American dramatic literature than Ridgeley [*sic*] Torrence's "Granny Maumee." It opened up entirely new fields.
>
> The audience at the Sunday night rehearsal, which was made up entirely of well known people, made the theatre resound with bravos after the curtain had fallen on the piece, and Dorothy Donnely, the principal interpreter (a white actress) was called before the footlights again and again.
>
> Mr. Torrence in "Granny Maumee" has written a serious play entirely about the negroes from the negro point of view. The whole

thing is as real, as fresh, as the beginning of the Irish theatre
movement must have been in Dublin.[12]

Of course, the critical acclaim must have been most gratifying
for the poet, but the excitement of the marriage and the production of *Granny Maumee* proved to be too large a strain on his
weak constitution. In May, Torrence was hospitalized for nervous
exhaustion. He and Olivia went to Xenia in late June, where they
stayed through the end of the year while he recuperated. During
this convalescence, Torrence continued to write poetry and to
gather material for his Negro plays. The poems were short lyrics
with settings inspired by his native Greene County. Like "Even-
song" and "Three O'Clock," they show a mastery of technique that
is seldom felt in his verse plays. These and other poems of the
period are discussed, however, in the next chapter.

Despite the impressive poetic output at this time, Torrence's
main goal was a professional production of *Granny Maumee* before it was forgotten. Harrison Grey Fiske, husband of the famous
actress, planned a production for April 19, 1915. The leading lady
was to be the French actress Mme Jolivet. Unfortunately, the production never materialized, but there was still hope. An audition
performance of the play was arranged for vaudeville bookers,
with the idea that the play would be booked as an attraction on
the major vaudeville circuits. Such a "road" production had a
precedent, as The Manhattan Players had presented *Granny
Maumee* at the Lyceum Theatre in Rochester, New York, in May,
1914, on a double bill with Frank Mandel and Helen Kraft's contemporary comedy, *Our Wives*. Once again, *Granny Maumee* received appreciative responses from the critics. The reviewer for
the Rochester *Evening Times* had this to say: "There is genuine
inspiration in Mr. Torrence's drama, its strength, its sense of mystery, its tragic intensity and its novelty making it one of the very
few real sensations of the year in the theatre." [13] The producers,
too, were happy with the results, but neither this success nor the
audition performance on the afternoon of April 22, 1915, seemed
to impress the two vaudeville bookers:

There were just two men who were to see it and judge and they
both came. They control the bookings. Well the fact is that the

blazing asses were too stupid to see the merit of the play and con-
sequently wouldn't offer Mr. Fiske enough per week to have it in
their theatres. They looked like a couple of gunmen and of course
that was their calibre. They were only used to judging the usual
vaudeville act consisting of slapstick men or trapeze performers or
trained animals and they frankly said that it was "beyond them."
. . . And this play has been delayed entirely through the stupidity
of those two vaudeville asses.[14]

So, despite the new recognition of Torrence the poet, the dramatist had to wait for his moment in the sun. Torrence and Olivia
were living at this time in an apartment at 107 Waverly Place, the
building owned by Harriet Moody. Mrs. Moody had given them
the apartment and financial aid, as she had done for many of her
struggling friends. A new opportunity came to them in the spring
of 1915, probably through the good offices of Robinson, when
Mrs. Edward MacDowell invited them to spend the summer at the
MacDowell Colony in Peterborough, New Hampshire. The colony
at Peterborough had already become the favorite summer home
of Robinson, who first visited there in 1911; by 1915, it was the
place where most of his creative work was accomplished.[15]

Torrence's visit to the artist's colony at Peterborough was cut
short by bad news from Xenia about the health of his father. Torrence returned home to be with his father during his last days (he
died on June 24) and to assist with the family business which was
eventually taken over by Ridgely's younger brother, Findley, who
also had held hopes of becoming a writer and who had to his
credit a large number of feature articles in one of the Dayton
papers.

The winter found Torrence back on Waverly Place working on
some new lyrics and making plans for the presentation of his
Negro plays. In February, 1917, he wrote his mother of a possible
production: "This afternoon I am expecting to go out to Groton to
talk over darky plays with Bobby Jones (Robert Edmond Jones)
who wants to put on the stage and costuming [sic] of some
pieces of mine."[16] It was not long before the plans made at that
discussion began to materialize. Torrence had four plays completed, but the actual production was not going to be easy. The
first problem was the assembling of a Negro acting company—a
difficult task, because few Negroes had entered the legitimate
theater as anything but musical performers, comedians, or stage

domestics. Harlem was obviously the first place to look for Negro performers: "I and my scenic man Robert Edmond Jones are going up to Harlem to attend a performance of colored people so that we may look over the ground." [17]

Despite the seemingly fertile ground of Harlem for casting a Negro play, Torrence and Jones found the task difficult. On March 2, Torrence wrote his family: "We have lots of discouragement in trying to assemble a company of colored people. We have the plays and Mrs. Hapgood [Emilie Hapgood, former wife of journalist Norman Hapgood, who invested in serious modern drama] has the money and readiness to hire a theatre and pay all expenses and Jones has his costumes and scenery designed but we are blocked so far by not being able to find the proper people available for casts." [18]

By March 12 things were looking up, but Torrence was still skeptical, as he wrote to Harriet Moody:

> I am still whittling at that proposed production of Negro plays but it is a long task and I don't know when the presentation will be made. At present we are still without a cast, two of the leading characters in one of the pieces are without actors to suggest them and we try out numbers of candidates every day. Meanwhile, two other plays are being rehearsed with fairly competent casts. But we are so far left in the dark as to whether we can make the production at all that we haven't had the scenery or costumes made yet.[19]

Still, the plays were ready to open at the old Garden Theatre on Thursday night, April 5, 1917. The preceding Sunday they had received an important advance notice from Robert Benchley in the New York *Tribune* in his article "Can this be the Native American Drama?":

> It may be that Thursday night will see the beginnings of a new movement on the American stage. Potentially, it is as rich in possibilities as any that have preceded it. It all depends on the spirit in which the public receive it. If they go expecting to see burlesque they will not only be disappointed; they will be ashamed. If they go with a sympathy for the attempt and an appreciation of its difficulties and aspirations, they may be witnessing the first stirrings of a really distinctive American drama.[20]

The three plays presented on that night were *Granny Maumee,* a folk tragedy obviously influenced by Synge's *Riders to the Sea;* a comedy, *The Rider of Dreams,* whose dreamer hero reminds one of Synge's Christy Mahon; and a historical pageant, *Simon the Cyrenian.* The performers came from just about every area except the Broadway "legitimate" theater. Some came from Negro companies such as the Lafayette in Harlem which played light drama, comedy, and musicals with Negro casts; others, from vaudeville and night clubs; and many had no acting experience at all. But under the painstaking direction of Robert Edmond Jones, the assembled cast appeared to be quite professional. Between the plays, a singing orchestra sang and played folk music and spirituals in such a compelling way that few people took advantage of the intermission.

There was unanimous enthusiasm for the plays, especially for *The Rider of Dreams.* The comments of Francis Hackett in *The New Republic* are typical of the enthusiastic reception afforded this lyrical little comedy:

> The way Mr. Torrence has caught the poet in his Rider of Dreams, has kept the rollick and lilt of Madison Sparrow without disturbing his innocence, is proof that with delicate art any kind of personality may be established on the stage. But in the intoxicated romance of Madison Sparrow, in the gallop of his imagination, there is no dependence on the popular idea of the Negro. . . . No one reared on the fodder of newspapers is prepared for such a burst of poetry, but the domestication of it by Mr. Torrence is as completely convincing as it is enchanting.[21]

Enthusiasm for the performers was more tempered. Hackett wrote that "Besides their gracious speech there is, despite much amateurishness, a real capacity for creating illusion." Alexander Woolcott was complimentary about the plays but less so about the players:

> Two of them [the plays] developed, from rich and almost entirely neglected material, such fine poetic and dramatic values that they fairly cried aloud for expression on the stage. One of them had been played here before, an unforgettable experience for the few who saw it. But when the hour came the plays were offered to

the public with a company of players who naturally looked the important roles to perfection, who made possible a most successful visual appeal, who were all you could ask in the matter of externals, but who, as it happened, had neither the endowment nor the training to express adequately the really big dramatic moments of the evening. These were blandly, almost complacently, forfeited.

It must be quite clear that the complaint here made against the decision of the producers was not that they decided to employ Negro actors, but that they decided to employ Negroes, whether they were actors or not.[22]

The plays moved uptown from the Garden Theatre to the Garrick on April 16 but survived there for only a week. An important factor in the failure of the plays at the box office may well have been the United States' declaration of war on the day after the plays' opening. With such momentous front-page news, few people probably bothered to read the reviews. Despite the lack of success, Torrence still had faith in the production: "It hasn't made a cent so far although it has been a great artistic success, that is, the papers have been unanimous in their approval and praise and all who have seen them have been enthusiastic but the audiences are slim. The thing is sure to go sooner or later but the time may not be ripe for it just now while the war is at this stage." [23]

For one critic, however, the declaration of war enhanced the power of one of the plays. Randolph Bourne wrote of seeing the plays on that eventful Friday:

It was Good Friday. And it was the day of the proclamation of war. As the solemn tones pealed out in the last play *Simon, the Cyrenian,* with its setting for the Crucifixion—"They that take the sword shall perish by the sword"—you could hear the audience catch its breath as it realized the piercing meaning of this heroic little drama of non-resistance played before a Christian nation that was going into a world war on the very day that its churches celebrated devoutly the anniversary of this very warning. . . . It seems imperative that no person with imagination miss this genuine dramatic experience.[24]

IV *The Plays*

Each of the three plays was unique not only in its treatment of
the life and attitudes of the Negro, but also in the form in which
Torrence chose to present his characters and themes.[25] The first
play, *Granny Maumee*, is a domestic tragedy; the setting is the
living room of an old Negro cabin that is dominated by a large
fireplace. Contrasted with the dinginess of the walls of the old
cabin are many touches of bright red: curtains, tablecloth, chairs,
geraniums. Here Torrence's predilection for color imagery has
been translated into effective visual terms.

Granny Maumee, who lives with her granddaughter Pearl, has
been blinded while trying to save her son Sam from being burned
alive by a white lynch mob. Since that time, a generation before,
she had been consumed by two passions: hatred for the white
man, and the desire for a male in the family to replace her lost
son. As the play begins, Granny is eagerly awaiting the homecom-
ing of her granddaughter Sapphire and the fulfillment of all
Granny's hopes, Sapphire's son. Sapphire arrives with her new
child, but the child is half white—the offspring of an illicit union
with the grandson of the murderer of Granny's son. For an instant
Granny's sight is restored, and she discovers the awful truth that
not only has the family's pure black blood been tainted but that it
has been mixed with the blood of murderers. Distraught, the old
woman loses her veneer of white man's Christianity and begins a
voodoo rite that culminates in the death of the white man who
tainted the blood of her family. During the rite, however, a vision
of Sam, Granny's son, appears to her and begs her to be merciful.
When Sapphire and Pearl awake from the stupor induced by the
old woman's potion, they find Granny dead.

We may readily see that there is too much dependence upon
coincidence for *Granny Maumee* to be a great play, but Torrence
presented his highly emotional plot with such skill that each moment is fully exploited. The setting, with its splotches of red, sym-
bolizing passion, blood, and fire, mirrors the highly passionate
nature of the superstitious old woman. Moreover, the entire action
of the play can be seen as a series of rituals. It opens with an
almost ritualistic presentation. The finest sheets are being placed

on the bed. Granny dresses herself in a red gown. Then comes the recognition scene in which Granny's sight is momentarily restored, and she sees the child's light skin. Finally, there is the highly dramatic voodoo rite with the two dazed granddaughters drumming in the background as Granny Maumee stabs the wax effigy of the white father of her great-grandchild. The scene builds to a fever pitch as the young women echo Granny's chants:

> By de w'ip an' de rope an' de chain dat swung,
> By de bloody mouf an' de bit off tongue,
> By de eat-up heaht an' de spit out gall,
> We scream, we beg, we whoop, we squall
> Tuh git poweh, tuh git stren'th tuh put de trick on um all. (27)

When the child's father arrives at the cabin door—the man Cranny wanted to burn as his grandfather had burnt her son—Granny cries from within: "Go back w'ite man. Roll back w'ite wave er de fiery lek. Once you lit de fieh an' bu'n me. Once you po' de blood an' pizen me, but dis time Sam an' me we's de stronges' an' we leaves you go, we leaves you live tuh mek yore peace wif Gawd. We're poure bloods heah, royal black—all but one an' we'll do de bes' we kin erbout him. He shill be name Sam. Go back w'ite man, an' sin no mo' " (30).

If the action proceeds in a ritualistic fashion, the language, too, is highly formalized. Torrence has attempted to use not only the Negro dialect, but also the simple colorful language and highly emotional nature of these people who were only one generation removed from the slaves when Torrence grew up. The language of the play is a result of Torrence's fine ear for the cadences of Negro speech as he heard it in and around Xenia.

We do not wonder at the enthusiasm *Granny Maumee* engendered at its first performance in 1914 and again in 1917, for this was the first time that a New York audience was presented with a picture of a Negro's bitterness toward the white man, much less a depiction as powerful as *Granny Maumee.* Granny's horror that the blood of her race would be tainted with white blood must have had a great deal of dramatic impact in 1917.

Just as *Granny Maumee* presents an embittered old woman at odds with the white world because of her desire for vengeance and her pride in her race, *The Rider of Dreams* presents a man whose conflict stems from his own irresponsibility. Madison Sparrow dreams of the wealth of the white man, but he does not have the energy to earn a decent living or the responsibility to hold on to the money his wife has saved to buy their house. His goal is that of the dreamer: "I goin' to lan' us all in a sof' place on dat Easy Street I heah' 'em singin' 'bout so long wifout seein' " (48). Madison, with the help of a white ne'er-do-well, has taken his wife's savings to buy a stolen guitar. Fortunately, their landlord, who resolves the problem as if he were a deus ex machina, has recovered the money and accepts it as full payment for the house. His only stipulation is that Madison use the guitar to his advantage: "I'm goin' to give you dat guitar—but—dere's suhtinly goin' to be a string tied to it. You kin take dat guitar but you got to make somethin' outer yourself wif her or back she'll come to me. You kin give lessons an' learn folks music or you kin write down de music you make, but you got to do somethin' wif it fer Lucy. You got to wake up or I'll take de guitar" (72).

We expect the play to end here, with everyone happy and all problems solved, but it does not. Madison Sparrow, the dreamer, is not that quick to accept the stringent requirements the world imposes upon him:

> I don' undehstan' dis worl'. If I wants to make music why can't folks lemme alone to make music? If I dream a fine dream why is it I always wake up? Looks to me like somebody's always tryin' to crown me out an' git me in a tight place.
> *Lucy* (his wife): . . . De trouble wuz dat dis dream of youahs wasn't a good dream.
> *Madison:* Yes, but not all of my dreams is bad ones. All I wants is room to dream my dreams an' make my own music. (75–76)

The critics liked *The Rider of Dreams* best, and it is not hard to understand why. Madison Sparrow's lyrical telling of his dreams makes it impossible for the audience to judge him harshly for his irresponsibility. He is a universal character, as old as comedy itself: he lies, he travels with the wrong people, he is constantly being duped, but he remains likable. A half-century before, he was a favorite character in the folk tales of the American Frontier, and, transferred again to the Negro world twenty years later, he became the irrepressible George "Kingfish" Stevens of "Amos and Andy." Unfortunately, the developing popularity of this type of character is partially a result of the white man's image of the Negro. Madison Sparrow, then, seems to us to be a stereotype; but his effectiveness is enhanced by the Negro setting of *The Rider of Dreams*. In it, we find a man who dreams of things he, as as Negro, cannot have; but the social implications of this problem are not explored in the play. It does not question the justice of Madison Sparrow's static position in society; rather, it operates within the existent framework of values. We cannot censure Torrence for this fact, for his interest in the Negro was more esthetic than social; moreover, his attitude was that of his time. In this context, the play remains a winning one.

Simon the Cyrenian provides a strong contrast with the other plays. A religious drama, it is set in the garden of Pontius Pilate on the day of Christ's crucifixion. The play is based on the verse from Saint Luke: "And as they led him away, they laid hold upon one Simon, a Cyrenian, coming out of the country, and on him they laid the cross, that he might bear it after Jesus" (Luke 23:26). Although we do not usually think of the characters involved in this incident as Negroes, Torrence's intention was that they should be depicted as such. His directions were explicit:

> Although Cyrene was in Northern Africa, the wall-paintings in the vast Cyrenian tombs depict black people instead of brown.
> That Jesus' cross bearer was a black man, as the early painters represented him, is a fact that holds a certain suggestion bearing upon a phase of modern society.
> It has been the author's design that all the characters in this play should be represented by persons entirely or partly of Negro blood; and this intention has been carried out in the original stage production. Simon is a full-blooded Negro, Battus is a little less dark, Acte is a mulatto as were most Egyptians of the latter dynasties. Her attendants comprise both mulattos and Negroes. The Roman characters are played by persons of a slighter Negroid strain. (78)

When the play begins, Procula, Pilate's wife, is disturbed because of the ominous dreams she has had regarding the consequences of Christ's crucifixion, and she has sent Simon, the leader

of the recent slave uprisings in Rome, to rescue Christ if he is
condemned. When Simon arrives, he discloses the fact that he is
already a believer in Christ:

> . . . I had summoned to a garden
> The bravest of the slaves to help them plan
> A new sedition that would free Barabbas.
> There as I roused the jungles against Rome
> I saw lights in another part of the garden,
> I saw men come with torches and seize a man.
> I hurried near and through the olive leaves
> His eyes looked into mine,
> His eyes burned into mine. I have seen them since,
> Waking or sleeping. (93)

When Christ is sentenced to death, Simon rushes to save him, but
he is transfixed when he sees Christ and hears Him speak: "Put up
the sword. For they that take the sword shall perish by the sword"
(108). Centurions take Simon and order him to carry Christ's
cross up the hill for him, and the play ends with Simon's being
taunted by the three mockers: The Mocker with the Scourge, The
Mocker with the Robe, and The Mocker with the Crown of
Thorns. As the crown of thorns is placed on Simon's head, Christ's
voice is heard once more: "If any man will come after me let him
take up the cross and follow me," to which Simon answers as he
takes up the cross: "I will wear this, I will bear this till he comes
into his own" (111).

Although it is difficult to know just exactly how much Torrence
intended to say in this short work, it certainly showed his belief in
the strength of human love and in pacifism; but it is difficult not to
see Simon as the oppressed Negro, just freed from slavery, accepting Christian love and pacifism as the only solutions to his problems. It may be, however, that Torrence only intended to say that
Christ spoke to Negroes as well as to whites—and that his message was, therefore, for both races.

Unlike the other two plays, much of *Simon the Cyrenian* is in
verse; but, unlike his earlier verse dramas, the meter is free; and
there is no attempt at rhyme. The result is a much more natural
flow of language. Like many religious plays, *Simon the Cyrenian*
shows a greater concern for the communication of an idea than
with logical motivation of character, and we feel that the mockers

contribute little to the effectiveness of the drama. The play's power, then, resides in its message—a message that was of particular import in April, 1917.

Torrence's *Plays for a Negro Theatre* were not great successes at the box office, nor was their subsequent publication by Macmillan profitable. Moreover, their lack of concern for the social, economic, and political position of the Negro in American society, and their acceptance of the Negro race as one apart from the mainstream of American life make them seem quite irrelevant to a reader of half a century later. Still, if the plays did not sound a battle cry, they did show an acceptance and a respect that the Negro had not yet been afforded in American society or on the American stage. They were a beginning for the Negro in our theater. For Torrence, they marked the culmination of all his dramatic hopes and efforts—a promise fulfilled.

CHAPTER *6*

Poetry, *The New Republic,* Robert Frost

Heaven gives its glimpses only to those
Not in position to look too close.
—Robert Frost, "A Passing Glimpse" [1]

I. *A Talent Matures*

THE second decade of the twentieth century marked Torrence's fruition as a literary artist. At the same time that he
established himself as an important figure in the history of the
American theater, he was carving for himself a secure place
among the major poets of his day. The poetry that Torrence wrote
between 1915 and 1920, which comprises the greater part of *Hesperides* (1925), represents Torrence's best work as a poet. However, Torrence's lyric poetry may seem anachronistic when seen
against its age; for Torrence can not be placed in the same category as Amy Lowell, Ezra Pound, or T. S. Eliot. But his mature
work is not hampered by the elevated diction and by the hedonistic themes of the late Victorian poets that had so strongly affected
his early works.

Like his late friend Moody, Torrence was interested in poetry
as a form of religious expression, as a means of communicating his
ideas concerning man's place in the world. His vision was not
timely—or modern—but it was concerned with the preservation
of the universal forces that raise man above a bestial level. His
poetry shows little of the effects of Darwin, Freud, or Spencer; for
man's fate is regarded as being dependent upon whether or not he
embraces universal love—a principle that negates all of the evil of
the world. Like the early Eliot, Torrence considered the world of
his age to be barren; but his bleak view was always countered by
the vision that could save man. His form in these poems is in no
way revolutionary, but he mastered the means not only of fulfill-

ing his early promise of giving his readers "something to chew on," but also of doing so in a lyrical verse that showed sensitivity and artistry.

All of these characteristics are evident in "A Vision of Spring," the first poem to appear in *The New Republic* that had made its first appearance on November 7, 1914. Torrence's poem, published in the issue of March 20, 1915, begins with the poet's looking out of his window and brooding upon his "wounded planet." As he looks out, he thinks that the return of spring will redeem the ugliness that he sees in a loveless world: "When grass rises again (I thought) the sorrow/Will lie hidden forever under beauty." [2] Suddenly, the poet's wish for the return of spring brings him a vision of the coming season, and he sees that his hopes will not be fulfilled: "But no healing was there; I saw none solaced,/Saw no comfort uplifted by the snowdrop."

With the vision, the poet hears the mournful song of spring: "I am flowerless, fruitless, for love has left me, / I am nothing without his breath to warm me." Only with the return of love as the prime force of earth will spring once again appear resplendent and the earth's wounds be healed:

> Unbelievably then would love inhabit
> All green places within the heart, outpouring
> Spring with thunder of her myriad fountains
> In one cup for the healing of the nations.

Here in free verse stanzas is a heartfelt plea for a world of love and peace—a plea that was most timely in those early days of World War I. Torrence's lines, though seldom end-stopped, often give a sense of being entities in themselves:

> Only weaponless, all forgiving, tender,
> Earth shall darken the skies no more with anguish,
> But with music and light shall move among them
> When the lands shall be only love-defended.

This stanza also demonstrates Torrence's predilection for a complex syntactical pattern combined with a rather simple vocabulary.

Torrence's poems of this period are often concerned with the common man rather than with the poet, and they have the folk quality that marked his Negro plays. "The Bird and the Tree," published in *Poetry: A Magazine of Verse* in April, 1915, is such a poem. The poem is addressed to a Negro in jail who is about to be lynched for a crime he did not commit:

> The sky is like a heavy lid
> Out here beyond the door tonight.
> What's that? A mutter down the street.
> What's that? A sound of yells and feet.
> For what you didn't do or did
> You'll pay the score tonight.[3]

In simple, rhythmic stanzas and simple language, Torrence mourns the injustice the Negro will suffer at the hands of the men who need "A white mask to hide the face."

"I Will Send the Comforter," published in the February 26, 1916, issue of *The New Republic* is interesting in its use of the dream vision and in its allusion to the golden apples of the Hesperides—both techniques that become characteristic of Torrence's mature verse. "I Will Send the Comforter" opens with a description of spring, the season of rebirth:

> April lit the apple-flower and waved it,
>   Music nested on the spray,
> Loudly called the lookout bird through rainbows,
>   Earth was curving into May.[4]

While in the midst of this orchard at spring, the poet is given a vision of the world of the spirit:

> Flashing seas beyond the melted skymark
>   Sang beneath another dome;
> There my vision sailed to breathless knowledge,
>   Sailed and found and drew back home.

The poet wakens from this vision eager to sing of his inspiration, but his earthly state makes such spiritual expression impossible:

> But the morning fell as leaves around me,
>   And the clay unpurified

> Mocked me, scourged me, till the dove-like glory
> Vanished from my wounded side.

One vision remains to the poet, that of the golden apples of the Hesperides, "raining from an immortal bough"; and the poet longs to bring this immortal, beautiful fruit, "Glorious for the hearts of men." At this point, the Comforter, the Divine spirit, speaks and reassures the poet that the spirit he seeks dwells within him:

> Deep within you sweep the burning splendors
> Brighter than your gaze can bear;
> There I watch among the dawns within you,
> Sky on sky is folded there.

Because of this indwelling of the Divine spirit, the poet is capable of translating his vision into poetry:

> Whoso suffers for my vision to bring it starlike
> Earthward out of dream at last,
> Bears the fruit and deepens homeward from the darkness,
> Holy sailor of the starry vast.

The poem is in quatrains and in characteristically simple but eloquent language. The quatrains are unified by the end rhyme of the second and fourth lines and by the insistent trochaic meter. The theme of "I Will Send the Comforter"—that of the indwelling of the spirit—is a result of Torrence's interest in mysticism that was particularly important to him at this time. He expressed his feelings and his idea for the poem in a letter to Harriet Moody:

> I am at present at work on a poem on the life of the spirit and it has quite caught me up. . . . The sense of suspension and delicate balance on earth seems to make it far more difficult than in other times to retain one's equipoise and the steadfastness of one's aim. On the other hand I suppose one might look upon life possibly as easier in that the very sense of weight that is now abroad in the world will drive the spirit to turn its gaze within and to follow the guidance found there toward a sense of mastery so that a still deeper and the only real security may be obtained.[5]

As "A Vision of Spring" stresses the renewing force of love, "I Will Send the Comforter" emphasizes the need for man to look within himself for the true source of his inspiration and strength. It is interesting, too, that Torrence used the golden apples of the Hesperides as his symbol for the goal of human aspiration. It seems likely that he derived this idea from Tennyson's poem, which describes the apples as "the treasure/Of the wisdom of the West." [6]

The February, 1916, issue of *The New Republic* contained "The Son," a simple folk poem that stands as Torrence's best known and most celebrated work, a work that deserves Louis Untermeyer's high praise: "Practically every anthology of the period contains 'The Son'—and yet I wonder how many of the readers are aware of the great artistry which has crowded the tragedy of a lifetime into so brilliant a condensation. Every casual line makes the revelation greater; every word is as starkly dramatic as it is inevitable." [7] The tragic tale of the loss of a beloved son, the memory of which is so inextricably linked with the life of the farm wife, is indeed expressed with great economy:

> I heard an old farm-wife,
> Selling some barley
> Mingle her life with life
> And the name "Charley."
>
> Saying: "The crop's all in,
> We're about through now;
> Long nights will soon begin,
> We're just us two now.
>
> "Twelve bushel at sixty cents,
> It's all I carried—
> He sickened making fence;
> He was to be married—
>
> "It feels like frost was near—
> His hair was curly
> The spring was late that year,
> But the harvest early." [8]

The woman's language is completely in keeping with her character, and the very terseness of her speech tells the reader a great deal. Torrence is using the people of his region with all the mastery that we find in Frost's depictions of the people of New England. Like Frost, though, Torrence's poems transcend their regional setting; for the feelings of subjects like the mother in "The Son" are universal.

"Eye Witness," which appeared in the December, 1916, issue of *Scribner's Magazine,* is one of Torrence's more ambitious lyrics; and, although not original in form or conception, it is also one of his most successful. The poem presents the song of a tramp which tells about his meeting with Christ—a meeting that taught the tramp the meaning of love. Torrence presents this theme with an admirable restraint that never allows the poem to lapse either into sentimentality or into easy truisms. The narrative that frames the song is in unrhymed verse with a varied meter, but the majority of lines are in a loose dactyllic pentameter. Characteristically, Torrence gives the poem unity through a heavy use of long vowel sounds and alliteration:

> There with the late light of the sunset upon them
> And on clear water spinning from a spring
> Through little cones of sand dancing and fading
> Close beside pine woods where a hermit-thrush
> Cast, when love dazzled him, shadows of music . . .[9]

In this pastoral setting, the tramp sings to his three companions, not of discontent, but of joy:

> There was no world there in the sky above him
> Deeper in promise than the earth beneath him
> Whose dust had flowered up in him the singer.

The song itself is presented in couplets, but in a simple language full of the type of similes that are characteristic of country people such as the people of Greene County, Ohio. Moreover, the syncopated rhythm of the couplets suggests folk songs or the calls for country dances. Torrence said he took the four-beat lines from the tramp ballads:[10]

> My heart went open like an apple sliced;
> I saw my Saviour and I saw my Christ.
> . . . .
> Told him I was weak as a rained-on bee;
> Told him I was lost.—Says: "Lean on me."

Christ's message to the tramp is the message of love, "The vinelike song with its winelike rain," the message that transformed the tramp into a singer:

> Oh, he took earth's pain to be his bride,
> While the heart of life sang in his side.
>
> For I felt that pain, I took its kiss,
> My heart broke into dust with his.
>
> Then sudden through the earth I found life springing;
> The dust men trampled on was singing.
>
> Deep in my dust I felt its tones;
> The roots of beauty went round my bones.
>
> I stirred, I rose like a flame, like a river,
> I stood on the line, I could sing for ever.
>
> Love had pierced into my human sheathing,
> Song came out of me simple as breathing.

After the tramp's song, he and his companions continue their journey:

> Then on the gilded track leading to the mountains,
> Against the moon they faded in common gold
> And earth bore East with all toward the new morning.

"Eye Witness" emerges as one of Torrence's most successful poems: the poet has complete control over his idiom; the simple language, which never seems coy, seems to flow naturally as the perfect medium for the poem's theme and setting and the technique of the dream vision is combined with the sound of the dialects of his region to present one of his most moving statements about the power of love.

Of course, much of the first half of 1917 was devoted to the production of the three Negro plays; but Torrence still found time to produce two poems. The first, "Survivors," was published in *Poetry: A Magazine of Verse* in January. Like "A Vision of Spring," "Survivors" mourns a land in which hate has replaced ideals and war has replaced love. The poem tells of an island inhabited only by hideous moths; for they are the only survivors: "Weapons and mouths they have, but little more,/And whoso-ever sees them, looks away." [11]

At one time the sky was filled, however, with beautiful butter-flies: "To beat against the floor of heaven and through,/And pour down daysprings gloriously bright." Their days were numbered, however, for a wind came and destroyed them, leaving only "the wingless, those who never dared," who "Went warm and safe and fat upon the ground:/And later, in due season, put forth stings."

In this parable, Torrence presents us with a world devoid of hope or aspiration—a world of creatures composed only of mouths and stings. The poem is presented in three six-line stanzas with a regular *abcabc* rhyme scheme, and the simplicity of pre sentation makes the poem's implications moving.

II *1917–1920: Years of Involvement and Opportunity*

The skepticism about the human condition that was expressed in "Survivors" was intensified for Torrence by America's entrance into the war in April, 1917. He and his wife were Pacifists, a dan-gerous choice of beliefs in times when jingoism seemed to rule the nation's sentiments. Of course, conscription was one of the main targets of the Pacifists' protests; and Torrence was actively op-posed to such a measure. In one of his letters to his family, he offers a vivid account of the action taken against the antidraft protests. While the details may be somewhat exaggerated, the letter attests to Torrence's horror at the prevailing militaristic spirit:

The feeling here is very high, whipped up by the irresponsible newspapers. Two of our girl friends have been arrested and jailed for proclaiming their peace sentiments by distributing little hand-bills about the size of one half of this letter paper. The bills only bore these words, "No conscription. Thou shalt not kill." This is all there was on them. The judge bound them over to the peace for six months. They were let off lightly because they wouldn't say in court that they meant to do it. The judge said that he didn't hold them on the words "no conscription" but the words "thou shalt not kill." He would have sent them to Blackwell's Peniten-tiary for the duration of the war if they had said they meant it. . . . There is already less free speech and other freedom in this part of the country at least than there has been in any European country for over a hundred years and it will get steadily worse.

At the recruiting tents on street corners they have phonographs playing the Star Spangled Banner and as citizens pass they have to take off their hats and if they don't a soldier steps up and knocks it off. If they object they are cuffed and beaten by other soldiers, perfectly irresponsible privates. No European country would tolerate such conditions and this is just the beginning.[12]

If anything, this exhibit of the petty in man strengthened Torrence's faith in the human spirit; for his letter to Harriet Moody expresses this position: "What a world it is these days and what a time for right thinking. There was never a time in the world's history when it was so apparent that the life of the spirit is the only true life. The other thing or the negation is daily disclosed."[13]

This belief in the need for a redemptive spirituality was transformed into art in his poem "Sea Dream," which appeared in *The New Republic* in November. The poem is based on a biological principle which Torrence states as the poem's epigraph: "The blood of man varies somewhat from the sea water of today, but approaches even more closely in composition the primal ocean out of which human life arose."[14] The sea of the poem, then, is the sea of life, the human bloodstream that is "Blood-blind with war and hate untold." However, unlike "The Survivors," "Sea Dream" is not a bitter poem; for the sea will return to its primal state:

> The foes, the fangs, the hates at last
> Buried in the water-mountain
> With the nations of the blind.

With this statement, the tone of the poem becomes one of exultation—a song of praise to the spirit:

> In the spirit, in the heart's deep places,
> Those hidden seas increase:
> The shining love from the eternal spaces
> That beats on earth with surges soft as fleece
> Fills them in silence from a tidal fountain,
> Until the golden day shall gleam
> When the red walls of hate are sealed,

Buried in the shining mountain
On the day of the heart's overflowing
When the earth is washed and healed,
And the lovers with the dream,
From ocean unto ocean going,
Shall lift at last into the living peace.

The human spirit, "that marvel in the body's dark," with its offer
of peace and love, can save man from the ravages of war—the
human spirit that is as much a part of man as blood and as much a
part of life as the sea which is the beginning of all life.

On November 8, 1918, the fateful meeting that ended World
War I was held in the private railroad coach on a siding near
Compiègne. Nothing proved the futility of the war more than this
armistice that was to have such tragic repercussions. Torrence,
whose Pacifist leanings were not lessened by the truce, wrote a
poem, "Peace," which was published in the Boston *Transcript* on
November 23. The regular *aabb* quatrains with their complex
meter underscore the urgency of Torrence's theme:

I hear in the night the echoing trouble of multiple drums;
Flutes lift their piercing fountains; a shadowy army comes,
The soldiers, the sailors, the banners and the brave,
For we have had a victory and they have had a grave.

I see in clouds the martyrs who burn above the mire—
The flowerlike, the towerlike, whom love led through the fire.
They die their deaths before me, beneath a broken sky;
They light earth's bloody pastures. I know their soundless cry:

"The house not made with hands once more is overthrown:
The old men's vision failed, the young men's dream has flown.
They turned upon their brothers, how shall they atone?
Wake to the field below where they have slain their own." [15]

Torrence's only other contributions in 1918 were the two poems
for children that appeared in *The New Republic* on December
28. The poems, "Invitation" and "Jean Singing," are written in
simple quatrains. The better of the two, "Jean Singing," is dedicated to Torrence's niece, of whom he was very fond. In this poem,
the singing of the young girl takes away the poet's sadness and replaces it with a real love for life:

> I shall remember the glory
> Filling this place
> The firebird calling through the rainbow:
> "Lift up your face."
>
> I shall remember how beauty
> Over death, over birth,
> Bridges a streaming music
> Here on the earth.[16]

In "The Apples," published in the March 3, 1919, issue of *The Nation,* Torrence presents his principal theme—that of the indwelling of the spirit—in the form of a myth. A wounded seaman, who is searching for an island with magical apples called "the mind's desire," finally nears the island and sees the tree laden with the enchanted fruit. After observing the splendors of the tree, the sailor calls out his wish:

> Bloody lands and flaming seas and cloudy slaughter,
> Hateful fogs unfurled,
> Steely horror, shaming sky and water,
> These have wreathed the world.
>
> Give me fruit for freighting, till my anchor grapples
> Home beyond the vast.
> Earth shall end her hating through the apples
> And be healed at last.[17]

But the solution to the world's hatred cannot be found outside of man, for the sea girls tell the sailor: "Beach and bough and dancers are within you,/There the island lies."

Man is again counselled to look within himself for the source of the love that will save mankind. The poem is comprised of fifteen quatrains with alternating long and short lines. The language is simple and straightforward, and the poem is a masterpiece of economy.

The Nation published another Torrence poem, "The Feasters," [18] in July. This two-part poem is about the plight of the American Indians and the Mexicans, both peoples persecuted and exploited by the Americans in their relentless march westward. The Indians, have been robbed of their land: "Having now their hunger only,/Going lonely on their quest/Toward the waters of the west." The five-line stanzas of the first part, "Pioneers and Indians," all too often remind us of Longfellow's "Hiawatha." The second part, "Mexican Plunder," is more successful. The two long stanzas bemoan the plight of the Mexicans at the hands of "the feasters," the greedy Americans. The imagery here is particularly vivid, especially in its picture of the bloody aftermath of the "feasters'" ambition:

> When they march, through raving hours,
> Breeding war to bear them dreams,
> When the nightmare foals with screams,
> Rolling on the bloody flowers,
> When a death shall save a trough
> Then the doom is not far off.

In September, 1920, Torrence began a year's tenure as a visiting professor of English at Miami University in Ohio. Professor Arthur Upham, an old friend of Torrence's, was going on leave and asked Torrence to take his courses in poetry and modern drama. This year was a happy one for Torrence, for he was close to his family in Xenia and even closer to his old friend Percy MacKaye, who was a writer-in-residence at the university. While at Miami, another appointment came Torrence's way when Walter Lippmann and Philip Littell invited him to become the poetry editor of *The New Republic,* the journal in which his work had frequently appeared. Torrence began the job immediately, as he could work from Miami without too much inconvenience. His job was to choose the poetry that appeared in *The New Republic,* and this assignment meant not only choosing from what was sent to the journal unsolicited but also inviting poets, both established and promising, to write for the journal. Instead of receiving a regular salary, Torrence participated in the profits of the magazine; and through this plan he received an average of $100 a month for his services.

Torrence was poetry editor for thirteen years, and he made *The New Republic* as potent a force in poetry as it was in politics. How Torrence's fellow poets felt about his appointment can be gauged by a letter from Carl Sandburg: "I wonder if I wrote you weeks ago as I ought to have done that I'm glad and doggone glad you're the Poetry Editor of *The New Republic.* If you stick on I'm going to send you stuff." [19]

Torrence's own writing did not stop when he became poetry editor. In November, 1920, *The Dial* published his lyric, "The Singers in a Cloud," another expression of the theme of the chaos of a strife-torn world that contrasts with the serenity of the spirit, symbolized by the placid blue sky. The world is darkened by the products of man's pettiness: "On the earth the battles war against light,/Heavy lies the harrow, bitter the field." [20] But above the world is blissful peace:

> Overhead is beauty, healing for the old
> Overhead is morning, nothing but youth,
> Only lovely youth.

Such optimism is easily scoffed at, but it gave Torrence a theme that inspired him to write his best verse—verse that ranked him with the best of his contemporaries.

III   *Robert Frost*

When Torrence returned to New York in 1921, he was able to devote more of his time to finding poetry for *The New Republic;* and it is not surprising that his work brought him closer to many of his fellow poets. Of course, he was still friendly with Robinson and Percy MacKaye, but many other figures began to be seen in Torrence's company. Chief among these was Robert Frost, who had mentioned Torrence in his correspondence as early as 1913. Their first intimate meeting was on March 3, 1919, when Frost dined with the Torrences at the apartment Harriet Moody had lent them on Waverly Place. Torrence described the meeting in a letter to Harriet Moody:

> Robert Frost came here to dinner last night. He called us up on Sunday and asked whether you were here and he was so disappointed to hear how narrowly he had missed you. He is certainly one of your most loyal appreciators. He agreed to come to dinner yesterday evening and we had a grand evening. . . . We had never had a real heart to heart talk with Frost before and we were quite carried away by him. He is surely one of the finest things that this country has produced. He is a man, a noble character in addition to being a noble poet.[21]

Frost's comment on the evening was, as would be expected, terse but to the point: "I had the good evening [*sic*] at your house in New York with the great-faced noble Ridgely." [22]

Actually, Torrence had been an admirer of Frost's poetry for years, for he had written Harriet Moody about the New Hampshire bard in December, 1915: "I don't know whether you are familiar with his work or not. I am not well versed in it myself but from the few things that I have lately read I have conceived a large regard for his reality and power. His poetry has come to stay and must be attended to. I feel sure of that." [23] Frost, of course, was happy to have his friend on the editorial staff of such an important periodical; and he was eager to answer Torrence's request for a poem. Torrence published the first of the poems Frost sent to him, "A Brook in the City," in the issue of March 9, 1921. Like Robinson, Frost also valued the opportunity to converse with his colleague: "I always keep seeing a light as I talk with him—and of course losing it as quickly; the thing is seeing it. He's some consolation." [24]

IV   Hesperides

During these years Torrence was devoting a good deal of time to preparing a volume of his poetry—a task that was long overdue. When the volume was published by Macmillan in 1925, it was entitled *Hesperides* after the first and longest poem. Very little of the volume was new—only "Hesperides" hadn't been published previously—but much of the earlier material had undergone minor revisions and all of it was worthy of publication in book form. The volume is a handsome one, though simple, bound in light green boards with an ivory-colored spine. The importance of *Hesperides* cannot be judged by the simple volume that houses it or by the relatively small number of copies that were printed.

The title poem is a development of the earlier poem, "The Apples." The technique again is a dream vision contrasting disillusionment with this world with a vision of a better world. Again, too, the central image is that of the golden apples. The poem begins with a young man, disillusioned, who stands in the city square: "When the trees that he stared among seemed of an evil wood/With a silence coiled at the root, aimed straight at the day." [25] Here it was hard to dream, hard to envision an ideal world. Suddenly the young man remembers a tale he once heard about the golden apples kept by the daughters of Hesperus. As he remembers, his memory turns into a vision:

> And he heard the pitiful sound of the city no more.
> For there in the street was the shining earth of the shore.
> And the walls of the street fell away to a long sea reach
> And a bough was over his head and he saw what it bore,
> For he stood in a golden shadow there on the beach
> Under the apples of life, a ripe world each.

But even this dream is not ideal and leads to disillusionment: "But he felt the weight of the apple all he could bear/And he tasted it,—bitter,—and let it fall to the ground." With this, the vision disappears; and the young man is again on the city street wishing that even this disappointing vision could return; but with this disillusionment comes the realization that the magical world he seeks is right there:

> But here where he breathed was the island, glittering-shored,
> By the sound of whose waters the songs were a shadow cast.
> And he saw at the street's end how it deepened at last
> Into the garden fed by the song and stream.
> So his vision had brought one thing from the waves he had passed,
> For his eyes held fast to the fire-like seed of his gleam;
> He had brought that back for the fruit of a better dream.

Louis Untermeyer felt that this poem contained "the mysterious ichor which preserves a few poems beyond their generation." [26] If time has not proved him to be correct, it has not dimmed the lyrical beauty of the poem in which we find all the characteristic traits of Torrence: the loose anapestic meter varied by an occasional spondee, the emphasis on long vowel sounds, and the internal rhyme. The result is a flowing, graceful style that is simple but never plain or commonplace; elegant but never ornate.

As we would expect, *Hesperides* was a critical success, but it did not add much to the Torrence coffers. In addition to the critical accolades was a very special type of praise from Robert Frost. After reading Torrence's volume, Frost dedicated a new poem, "A Passing Glimpse," "*To Ridgely Torrence/On Last Looking into His 'Hesperides.'*" The fact that this poem was the only time

Frost made such a gesture enhances its place as one of the highest honors Torrence received during his career.

These years, from 1915 to 1925, were the high point of Torrence's career, for the three Negro plays had made an important contribution to the history of the American theater, and the poems in *Hesperides* are proof of the high place Torrence merits in American poetry. His poetry, as represented in this collection has come a long way from the highly ornate echoes of Swinburne that Torrence wrote at the beginning of his career. Gone, too, is the forced quality of the all-too-elevated verse of the poetic dramas. What replaces it is a style that is simple, economical but highly distinctive. The language is natural, but it is given a lyrical quality by Torrence's heavy use of long, open vowel sounds and dancing meter: "Down by the railroad in a green valley/By dancing water, there he stayed awhile." The effect of this style is one of a smooth lyric flow from one line to the next. One is conscious of the movement of the line but only as an organic part of the total effect of the poem.

If the *Hesperides* poems show a mastery of technique, they also are obviously the work of a perceptive, sensitive intellect that is sympathetic toward the problems of his fellow men and that believes strongly in his solution—love and faith in the greatness of the human spirit. His favorite method of presenting his theme seems to be the juxtaposition of the real with the ideal, often through the use of a vision. What Torrence's characters usually discover is that the beauty they seek must be realized within themselves before they can see it in the world. To apprehend beauty, man must be spiritually "beautiful," and this spiritual beauty comes from the realization of his innate capacity to love.

The critical reception for *Hesperides* was close to ecstatic. Untermeyer entitled his review "Achievement," and this word seemed to reflect the general attitude toward *Hesperides*. Torrence's first volume of poetry since *The House of a Hundred Lights* fulfilled the promise demonstrated in that volume. Torrence had mastered his craft, and he had moved to the top rung of contemporary American poets.

CHAPTER 7

The Last Quarter Century

Torrence was unobtrusive: a slim and in his later days almost cadaverous person of medium height, or a little more; sallow skin, blue eyes, I seem to remember, a very high forehead with the hair receding further and further, except for a few grey-blond strands pulled over the expanse of baldness. I remember him holding out a manuscript with a very long hand. . . .[1]

I *Resignation*

ALTHOUGH the last twenty-five years of Torrence's life might have seemed like a creative twilight after the activity that had filled the preceding decade, these years were not marked by inactivity. First there was the continuation of his job as poetry editor of *The New Republic*. So excellent was Torrence's work in this post that an English critic, L. A. G. Strong, has said that "A tired anthologist, if pushed for time, might publish everything in the 'New Republic' and know he had no bad poetry." [2] Torrence, quite selective, rejected nine tenths of what was submitted. While part of this high selectivity was a result of Torrence's standards, much of it was dictated by considerations of space. Poetry was not the main concern of *The New Republic;* and, while the editors were interested in quality, quantity was a problem as the poetry was used merely to fill blank spaces. Torrence customarily left his final selections with Betty Huling, who was in charge of makeup, and she would use them when the right space was available.

Torrence resigned from his post as poetry editor in 1933; conflicting reasons for his resignation have been offered. As Torrence explained the situation, he had full authority over the choice of poems until Bruce Bliven replaced Herbert Croly as editor. Bliven, who wanted to have some say in the selection of poetry for the journal, told Torrence that Mrs. Willard Straight, one of the founders of *The New Republic,* wanted to publish the work of newer poets such as W. H. Auden and Stephen Spender. Torrence knew that Mr. Straight was a self-styled expert in poetry— and an Englishman—and was undoubtedly behind this request. He acquiesced and wrote Auden and Spender for poems and printed them. When Straight and Bliven kept giving him names, however, Torrence finally felt that he did not want to continue under such conditions.

The readers of *The New Republic* noticed the difference in the poetry printed after Bliven became editor. Some of these readers, such as Carrie Clive Bliss, let their feelings be known to Bliven: "It has been very disappointing to your readers who are interested in verse, to notice the deterioration of this section of the magazine. For the last two years there has been a steady falling off in quality, and a swinging toward the sickly, the obscure, the intricate and labored. . . . Where's the man who used to buy your poetry. You can't tell me he picked these." [3] It is not surprising that Torrence chose to resign when the quality of work for which he was responsible diminished because of outside interference.

Torrence's explanation of his leaving *The New Republic* makes sense, but so do the reasons offered by Bruce Bliven and Malcolm Cowley. Bliven says that "We were printing so little verse that neither we nor he thought it was worth while to continue." [4] Malcolm Cowley, who assumed Torrence's position as poetry editor, offers much the same explanation: "Then in the middle years of the depression *The New Republic* was hard up and the editors decided that they couldn't afford having a poetry editor, so that the task of accepting a few poems devolved on me. It is painful now to think that I replaced Torrence through no design of my own, for the small weekly salary he received must have played a part in his budget." [5]

Whatever the reason was for his leaving, Torrence's service during his thirteen years as poetry editor of *The New Republic* was highly respected by poets and readers alike. Typical of their feelings about his work was the statement of poet Rolf Hum-

phries: "I should like to express not only for myself, but also—if it
is not presumptuous—for others who contributed poetry to The
New Republic from 1920 to 1933 our appreciative consciousness
of Mr. Torrence's service to poetry in his editorship during those
years. He helped us all, a great deal; but that was only part of
it." [6] Bruce Bliven also offers an interesting assessment of the place
of poetry in *The New Republic* during Torrence's years as poetry
editor:

> I liked Ridgely very much, and so did everyone else who worked
> with him. He was an authentic, though minor, talent as a poet,
> and his taste in poetry seemed to me excellent. . . . Our prob-
> lem was trying to make room for poetry at all, in a magazine
> primarily trying to cover the world news of politics, economics
> and social history. Looking back, I now wish we had worked
> harder to get in more verse, tho as you know, the years of his
> editorship, 1920 to 1934, were not very fruitful in the arts. His
> tastes were rather conventional, and so were ours, and we did not
> do much with avant garde poetry, which had flourished around
> 1915 and was to flourish again a decade or two later.[7]

II *Some Grave Losses*

Torrence did not do much writing of his own during the decade
that followed the publication of *Hesperides*. A great amount of
his time, of course, was spent with his editorial work; but it is
likely that the lack of popular success of *Hesperides* hampered his
motivation. Still, his work during the preceding years had given
the Torrences enough money to purchase two houses on Morton
Street in Greenwich Village, from which they received a modest
income by renting out most of the space, saving only one floor for
themselves.

The early 1930's were marked not only by Torrence's loss of his
position at *The New Republic* but also by the loss of two of his
dearest friends. In February, 1932, Harriet Moody, that coura-
geous woman who had meant so much to so many artists, died
suddenly of an attack of asthma. Mrs. Moody's name has appeared often in these pages, for she seemed to have replaced her
husband in becoming Torrence's confidante. He unfolded his innermost thoughts to her as he did to no one else. He shared with
her a faith in the unknown and a strong faith in love and the

human will. Harriet was more than a spiritual companion, however; she provided material assistance of many kinds in addition to the apartment on Waverly Place. It was fitting that Torrence should have been chosen to write her memorial in *The New Republic*.

The other loss was an even greater one for American letters. In the middle of January, 1935, the tall, gaunt poet from Gardiner, Maine, Edwin Arlington Robinson, was admitted to New York Hospital. In March, the doctors discovered a cancer that was too far developed to be operable, and he died on April 6. Torrence was his constant companion at the hospital, helping him with the proofreading of *King Jasper* and trying to keep him cheerful, a task Torrence had assumed in 1900. As usual, Robinson saw the dark side of everything. When Torrence commented on the fine view the hospital window afforded, Robinson said that he could not stand the view because he could see Welfare Island, where the poor old men were living in dingy quarters while he was enjoying so much attention in his fine hospital room.

Chard Powers Smith, in his biography of Robinson, gives a touching picture of Torrence's last visit to New York Hospital: "Ridgely and E.A. were both tall and lean, and seem to have required vests with eleven buttons instead of the ten that had been orthodox in the nineties when they were young. When Ridgely last saw E.A., he was too near coma to speak. But he was able to lift his hand, and what might have been the last gesture of that long first finger was to reach up and, starting at the top, to go through the motion of counting the buttons downward, slow one after one." [8]

Robinson was not only a friend but also an admirer, and for Robinson to express admiration of a colleague's work was something of an honor. Hagedorn notes that Robinson raged when Torrence was not granted the Pulitzer Prize for *Hesperides*. His admiration was given tangible form when he dedicated *Matthias at the Door* to Torrence in 1931. Because of the length and intimacy of their relationship, we would think that Robinson would have wanted Torrence to write his official biography but he had desired that Edwin Carty Ranck write it. Whether Torrence declined the honor, or was not asked, is not clear; but he did serve Robinson's memory in another important way. In 1940, with the help of Hagedorn, Ledoux, and Isaacs, Torrence edited a selection of Robinson's letters. While the edition is by no means complete—Torrence was especially reluctant to print the letters that Robinson had written him—it presents an interesting picture of one side of Robinson, the man who, Torrence said, "made a cult of friendship." [9] Torrence's fine introduction reflects his fondness for E.A.R.:

> But what if posterity, in spite of him, should turn from his poetry to his letters in search of his human quality? Such natural curiosity will not go unrewarded. Indeed posterity, if it pleases, will know far more about him than was known during his lifetime, when brief impression and popular report labeled him a shy New Englander whose writing out-soared his speech as the lark the snail. This in fact was true, part of the time. But if he was a poet, first of all, he was also emphatically a human being, and not all his reticence can keep his letters from revealing the warmth, genuineness and variety of his human relationships.[10]

With Harriet Moody's death many American artists lost a great friend and supporter; and, with the death of Robinson, American poetry lost one of its finest voices. The loss was deeply felt by Torrence, who had been close to both of them since the early days of the century. He had been the recipient of the generous aid of Mrs. Moody, and the giver of moral support to Robinson.

III   *Renewed Inspiration*

Despite the grief he suffered from the loss of two of his closest friends, Torrence began to write once again. The new abundance of creative output that began in the mid-1930's was in the area of poetry, not drama. Torrence's dramatic career never flourished after the Negro plays. *The Rider of Dreams* had been performed in Paris in December, 1928, on a bill with O'Neill's *The Emperor Jones*. Torrence's play, with its companion pieces, was given a number of amateur performances in the 1920's and 1930's, but Torrence found it impossible to duplicate its success. During the 1930's he worked intermittently on a play about Goya, but the play remains an unfinished manuscript. He admitted in 1936 that "I have never got the plot arranged to suit me." [11] He wrote a one-act play about Thomas Paine, *Common Sense*, which was released for amateur performance by Dramatists' Play Service in 1942, but it earned only $1.29 in royalties during its first year.

The quality of the poetry Torrence wrote in the late 1930's makes the ten-year silence after *Hesperides* more inexplicable, for the later poetry is as good as the fine work that had constituted his earlier volume. Whether it was the break with *The New Republic* or merely a renewed desire to write poetry that led to this new work cannot be ascertained, but once again Torrence's poetry was being read. "Outline," published in *The Saturday Review of Literature* on May 30, 1936, was his first poetic appearance in over a decade. The poem is a simple, quiet piece, written in *abab* quatrains. The meter is more regular than that which Torrence used in his earlier work. There is no moral—no attack on the cruelty of man or affirmation of love—but "Outline" does contain the type of quiet tragedy that characterized "The Son." In three stanzas, a drama in miniature is presented:

> There was longing on the beach.
>   There were certain broken words
> Mingled, to the end of speech,
>   With the watersong of birds:
>
> "Wait" and "yes," and he was gone.
>   Distance waved a fading hem.
> Then the shore she stood upon
>   Faced the years that sundered them.
>
> Back he came, the world-beguiled,
>   To the sands where youth had clung.
> But the shade that waited, smiled
>   The smiling of the too long young.[12]

The next year, 1937, Torrence was elected chairman of the Academy of American Poets, an organization he had helped found in 1934. The academy actually began when Mrs. Hugh Bullock decided that American poets suffered not only from a lack of public recognition but also from the financial discomfort that was its consequence. She enlisted the aid of Edwin Arlington Robinson, Louis Ledoux, Torrence, and a number of others to organize the academy. A New York State charter was granted in 1934, and the academy began with five founder-members, Mrs. Bullock, Torrence, Mr. and Mrs. Joseph Auslander, and Charles Hanson Towne. Its cause was explicit: "To encourage, stimulate, and foster the production of American poetry by providing fellowships for poets of proven merit, by granting scholarships, awards and prizes for poetic achievement, and by such other means as the Board of Directors with the approval of the Board of Chancellors may from time to time devise and determine." [13]

Torrence and Olivia worked indefatigably for the academy, by producing pamphlets to explain the urgency of its cause and by contacting many prospective donors. During the first year of Torrence's chairmanship, the academy granted its first $5,000 fellowship to Torrence's old friend, Edwin Markham.

In May, 1937, *The New Republic* published two new poems by Torrence. Both resume one of Torrence's main themes—the cruelty and destruction of war. The theme was once more timely, for Hitler's Germany had reached out a greedy and vengeful hand to prove that it was not to be defeated by any treaties. "Europa and the Bull," turns the old myth into a prophecy of the outcome of the impending war. The poem, a sonnet, bears more than a casual resemblance to Yeats's "Leda and the Swan," but Torrence's poem is less symbolic and more overtly emotional. The poem begins with a frightening picture of Zeus's pursuit of Europa:

> Strayed from what meadow of hell this bellowing shape
> To her who sees the figures of her dread
> Stem from the belly and from out the head
> And sees the hoofs beneath the lowered nape
> Plunge, as she seeks in earth and sky, escape? [14]

But the rape is inevitable, as is its fruit, "half beast, all monster," who carries the seeds of his own destruction:

> Whoever lives and still has eyes unharmed
> May see at last the hoof-like feet stamp out
> The torch of mind, man's dream, to the last spark.

For Torrence, the fruit of the forced union of Zeus and Europa is war; and this terrible progeny is about to wreak its worst destruction. "Europa and the Bull," characteristically, is effective in great part because of its economy. Torrence has presented his mythic nightmare in the most simple form possible. The emotional impact is intensified by the long vowel sounds and by the insistent iambic pentameter.

In "Men and Wheat," another poem about the ravages of war, the battlefield, scattered with the bodies of the dead, is compared to a field of ripening wheat. The poem is in *abab* quatrains with a complex metrical scheme that alternates iambs and anapests. The effect is an insistent rhythm that emphasizes the horror of the poem's theme:

> The sheaves of men lie flat
> And are buried where they bleed.
> But what dread food is that?
> And what mouths does it feed? [15]

With Torrence's renewed poetic activity came renewed recognition. In June, 1937, Torrence's first college, Miami University, awarded him an honorary Doctor of Letters. Later that month Torrence returned to another scene of his college days, Princeton University, to join his class for its fortieth reunion. His old friend from Xenia, Austin Patterson, was his constant companion during a weekend that renewed an association with Princeton that had been broken since that bleak December day in 1896. This reinstatement of an old tie was welcomed by both sides, and Torrence's renewed association with the university led to some highly valued acquisitions for the Princeton University Library. Torrence's portrait occupies a prominent place in the library's poetry room, not only in recognition of his poetry, but also in honor of his friendship and generosity.

Another result of Torrence's return to the Princeton campus was his visiting professorship at Antioch College for the spring term of 1938. Austin Patterson, at that time the vice-president of Antioch, had approached Torrence with the invitation at reunions, and Torrence eagerly accepted the opportunity to teach at another Ohio college. Torrence's teaching activity must not have allowed him much time for poetry, for his next work, "On Storm King Edge," did not appear until June, 1939. This, too, is a poem about the horror of war which can destroy all that man and nature have created—war which is a result of those with ways "that turn aside from pity;/The ways of those who take the sword/And on the victim build their city." [16] The poem is in quatrains with an irregu-

lar meter and an *abcb* rhyme scheme. Unfortunately, this rel-
ative lack of pattern gives the poem a rambling quality that emphasizes its didacticism.

Torrence's continuing interest in the problems of the American
Negro, particularly the Negro artist, was rewarded by a grant
from the Rockefeller Foundation which enabled the poet to study
the Negro theater in America. His base of operation was the famous Karamu Theatre in Cleveland, the oldest legitimate Negro
theater in the United States. Torrence was interested in finding
the nature and quantity of plays written by Negroes and in en-
couraging gifted Negro playwrights to continue their work. This
study involved a great deal of correspondence and reading of
manuscripts, all of which Torrence executed admirably. In addition, he compiled a complete bibliography of plays by American
Negroes. His report on his research presents a penetrating analysis of the problems of the Negro dramatist of his time. In addition
to comments on the problems of the playwrights, Torrence makes
some cogent comments about the audiences for Negro plays:

> Another great need of the Negro theatre is to secure more edu-
> cated audiences. This lack will undoubtedly be supplied by the
> enlightening effect of more and better plays, but at present the
> difficulty in regard to some audiences presents something of an
> impasse. In their choice of plays for presentation drama directors
> in some of the Negro colleges find themselves greatly restricted by
> the character of their publics. Not only must they consider the
> prejudices of the local population, both white and colored, but
> they are often hampered by the conventionality and timidity of
> their own trustees and authorities.
>
> In addition there is among some audiences in such localities a
> great reluctance to see or hear certain aspects of reality concern-
> ing their own lives. Many of them do not wish to see the Negro
> in his racial distinction presented at all on the stage. They prefer
> to see him only playing the part of a white man in classic plays.
> Others prefer to see him presented only as a hero. The existence
> of such a psychology reveals of course the deep necessity for the
> very kind of education the theatre affords.[17]

During the course of his study of the Negro theater, Torrence
met a number of the leading Negro educators. Of course, he had
been admired by Negro leaders for a long time because of his in-

terest in the Negro, not only as a dramatic subject, but also as a member of an underpriviledged minority group. He had supported such organizations as the NAACP, and he was concerned with the problem of properly educating the growing Negro population. This study for the Rockefeller Foundation was not to be the last product of Torrence's interest in the American Negro, as we shall see.

While Torrence was in Cleveland working on his research for the Rockefeller Foundation, he also was writing five short poems which were published in *Poetry: A Magazine of Verse* in November, 1939. The poems are varied in form and subject matter, but they are linked by Torrence's familiar themes: the horror of war and the strength of love and the human will. Characteristically, there is much use of light and dark and of sight imagery. "This Light" begins with a questioning of the philosophy that the real life is that which comes after death, and the poem ends with an affirmation of the one life that we know—that which we have on earth:

Yes this earth, yes this love, joy and grief for the lover,
Yes these orbs, hours, faces, these dreams that a dream may
    recover.

Here clouded, forever half-lost between triumph and doom
Night-islanded life, unquenched, slowly widens its room

With beacons, with dawns that unveil it, the hidden and strange,
As it lifts from the steadfast tides of the ocean of change,

With rays on footholds gaining to summits more proud
And won more surely than under a sky without cloud,

And better than any escape to a sky apart
Are gleams from the heights to the shadows that lie in the heart.[18]

As in the earlier "Hesperides" and "Legend" the reader is told that the happiness he seeks can only be found within himself in this life and not in any visionary world. The poem is in rhymed couplets, and the meter returns to the seemingly loose structure of the earlier poems.

"The Watcher" and "Harvest Home" are war poems similar to

"Men and Wheat" in their use of a simple quatrain form and what might be called "agricultural imagery," as well as in their emphasis on the horrors of war. In the last two poems of the series —"Heard from a Dark Stage" and "Adam's Dying"—Torrence replaces his favorite device of the dream vision with a conflict between a man and his memory. In "Heard from a Dark Stage," the poet's memory wishes to snare him in a trap of remorse, guilt, and woe for his days "lived and lost." The poet, however, refuses to be snared:

> Deep then, in my broken earth
> I'll bring other seed to birth.
> Out of it I'll seize and shape
> Life the vine, and love the grape.
> In them, through those veins I'll pour
> Myself, my being, to its core.
> The vine of life, that twining gleam,
> Shall bear me in its upward stream,
> Bear my mind of fire and dream,
> The burning fruit the fiery tide
> From the heart within my side.
> Fire to fire, I shall have passed
> Free, triumphant at the last,
> Rising, as the vine ascends,
> Free, before the end of ends.

Despite the potential for evil that Torrence so eloquently ascribes to man in the war poems, "Heard From a Dark Stage" admonishes man not to be crippled by past wrongs but to embrace the principles of love and life so as to enrich the future. Torrence was always more successful at presenting the positive side of his philosophy, and the simple rhymed couplets and regular meter of this poem are far more effective than the lumbering form of "On Storm King Edge."

"Adam's Dying" presents an interesting variation on the same theme. The poem tells of Adam's last thoughts—his painful memories of remorse and punishment are countered by the pleasant memories of the joys of life and love. Despite Adam's sin and its effects on his descendants, the poem suggests that Adam's last memories should be of his most joyous moments:

        The sky's dome,
            The sun's west,
        A man's home,
            Eve's breast.

        The wave's beach,
            The bird's wood,
        Dreams each,
            But all good.

        Life finds rest
            Where life rose.
        Which was best?
            The heart knows.

The *abab* quatrains, with their lines of two feet, give the reader a sense of the fleeting impressions that race across Adam's mind before his death.

This same preoccupation with the mind's merging of past, present, and future was manifested in one of Torrence's most celebrated poems, "Lincoln's Dream," which appeared in *The New Republic* in February, 1941. The long blank-verse poem presents Lincoln's thoughts as he suddenly awakened from that fateful dream of Good Friday morning, 1865. It begins with his description of the dream:

                    The Form lay there
        With the face covered. Hid. But not from me.
        I knew it. Who knew better? There I lay.
        "The President is dead." No need to say so.[19]

Lincoln then thinks back to similar presentiments that he had had as a boy:

                And I have seen them since
        And not less real than anything on earth
        Seen with the outward eye lighted by reason.

In the third part of the poem, Lincoln speaks of his other recurring dream:

> Once more on board that dim mysterious deck,
> Fixed like a part of it and sensing only
> Darkness, the hid wheel and the helmsman hidden
> And prow set into darkness as the ship
> Moves with a giant force through the dark water,
> Swift to an unknown shore.

He relates this ship to the Ship of State and speaks of America's
course—first the warlike course of the recent past:

> Antietam, Gettysburg,—but in the end
> What did those victories cost us? Young men dead.
> Dead. On both sides. The nation's life. The flower
> And in a war that never would have been
> But for blind pilots long before it struck.

Then he foresees the fearsome way of the future:

> But beyond all that threatens, all that strikes,
> Whatever shadows, bolts, disasters, dooms
> Loom from the sea or air to bring her down,
> None are so dangerous as those within.

The poem is a powerful statement of Torrence's beliefs beautifully set within his topic. The natural flow of language, devoid of
any artifice, is a perfect medium for his subject.

The verse that Torrence wrote between 1936 and 1941 deserved
publication in book form; and Macmillan, who had published
Hesperides and the Robinson letters, issued *Poems, by Ridgely
Torrence* in the early fall of 1941. The attractive blue volume
contains the *Hesperides* poems, the poems discussed in this chapter, and three additional poems: "Prothalamium," "Songs from a
Story," and "The Word that Walked Among the Ancient Trees."
The first of these new poems is a simple lyric in quatrains that
urges the bride to marry despite the war so that she may help
bring forth a better generation. The "Songs from a Story" are two
short lyrics—one a quatrain, the other a mere triolet—on the inev-
itability of the passage of time. The third new offering is on a
larger scale, and the title "The Word that Walked Among the
Ancient Trees" is taken from William Blake's *Songs of Experience*.
The work actually contains two poems. The first, "Night Song,"

is a hymn to God—or "Life" as Torrence addresses him—asking
him to bring back the day that man may "see and learn to bear
the light." As in the "Songs from a Story," a sense of the inevi-
tability of death pervades the poem:

> For all our days are ended in one fate,
> Our time, our utmost years, a piteous stay.
> Our years are like a cobweb wiped away
> Or like a bitter pathway found too late,
> Reaching through darkness where we grope and sigh
> To the dark ending into which we fly.[20]

The second poem, "Adam's Song of the Visible World," is a ju-
bilant hymn of praise and thanksgiving to the "Source of Life."
Torrence had seldom written such a joyful work, for we find no
mourning for the cruelty of war, no sense of the imminence of
death, only the happiness of enjoying life:

> What life! What splendors in how many shapes
> Are in this world, O Source, who made them all!
> And with what wisdom made them, great and small!
> Even their number on the earth escapes
> Dreams or imaginings. The earth is full. (45)

The poem ends with a strong statement of faith and a re-ded-
ication:

> You are my tide of joy, my sea, my shore,
> My field of sky with stars that never set,
> And I will learn your wonders all my days,
> Let me remember you and let
> The spirit of denial vanish quite
> From earth and be forgotten in its ways,
> And my blind ways in darkness be no more. (47)

Again, Torrence uses blank verse as his medium, and it is interesting to note what a strong emotional impact he can achieve
with the simplest possible language. There are few words of more
than one syllable, yet Torrence uses such a vocabulary in a most
sophisticated manner.

The publication of this new volume offered the critics another opportunity to express their admiration for Torrence's work. Rolf Humphries' review in *The New Republic* is one of the longest and most favorable:

> Reading the poems in this book, one must admire the poet's serenity, candor, trueness, devotion. His line is always clear and musical, the tone sure, the accent right. This clarity gives Mr. Torrence's work a satisfactory timelessness; he can be modern without being modish; neither is he unaware of the bardic tradition. This tradition imputes no reproach to the poet if he is called, at times, "inspirational," at others "visionary," or "dreamer." It is a tradition in which the general may prevail over the particular; it permits occasional vagueness, along with largeness, of mood or image; it skirts, at its lower levels, oratory or rhetoric; at its higher reaches, it approaches prophecy. It draws the poet on to raptness, exaltation . . . the total worth of the book exceeds the sum of its parts, for it establishes communion with a fine poet and a spirit at once perceptive, humane and reconciled.[21]

Louis Untermeyer began his evaluation in the *Saturday Review of Literature* by regretting that Torrence had written so little—that the new volume contained so much that was not new —but he concluded with a positive judgment of the collection:

> On the affirmative side there is the discrimination which denies publication to anything meretricious. The very restraint which limits the expression of a lifetime to thirty-four poems emphasizes the tensity of "The Bird and the Tree," that unforgettable poem of a lynching; "The Singers in a Cloud," one of the finest lyrical poems of the period; "Eye Witness," an evocation of the second coming of Christ seen through the eyes of a tramp; and "The Son," which packs a life tragedy in sixteen lyrical lines. That these poems are not new is anything but an unfavorable fact; the familiarity, due to constant quotation, is a proof of their condensed and dateless power.[22]

In 1952, the volume was reprinted. This edition of *Poems, by Ridgely Torrence* also contains two new poems—the only two works he completed during the last nine years of his life.[23] "Knife Song" is a folklike chant against death inflicted by war.

The other work, "Ygdrasil," was published in the *Saturday Review of Literature* on September 7, 1946. Ydgrasil, in Scandinavian mythology, was a giant tree whose roots stretched out and supported the universe. It was fitting that this, Torrence's last published poem, should be his most eloquent plea for peace:

> On one sole ground will the world-tree flourish,
> On earth unarmored against its bearing,
> Its glories free and its strength to nourish
> The world wide lands in a common sharing.
>
> In kinship only, with all earth gardened,
> The ravished leaf may be stayed in thinning,
> The stony ground at the root unhardened,
> The bough be green in a new beginning.[24]

IV *The Final Work*

If Torrence did not devote much of his energy to poetry in the last decade of his life, he did not stop working. His last years were spent with two of his favorite interests: the cause of the American poet and that of the American Negro. He was unflagging in his devotion to the Academy of American Poets. As we have observed, he and Olivia wrote a good deal of promotional material for the academy and worked at raising funds to sustain its fellowships. No awards were made during the war years, but the academy was able to continue offering awards to worthy poets in 1946 when it gave its $5,000 fellowship to Edgar Lee Masters. The recipients of the fellowship were chosen by a ballot of the academy's chancellors, which at the time included Archibald MacLeish, Robinson Jeffers, and William Rose Benét. The next year, 1947, the chancellors designated Torrence as the recipient of the fellowship—and few honors could have meant more to one of the Academy's most devoted servants. In 1950, Torrence was elected to the Board of Chancellors, a post he did not hold for long because of his death.

Much of Torrence's time during the 1940's was spent speaking to college groups. The colleges he addressed included not only Miami, where he spent another term in 1942, and Harvard, but also a number of Negro colleges where he renewed several friendships that he had made while working on his study of the

Negro drama. One of the products of his close ties to the Negro colleges was a grant from the Carnegie Corporation, given through Atlanta University, to write *The Story of John Hope*.[25] Torrence worked long and hard obtaining every possible shred of information about the distinguished Negro educator.

John Hope's story is one of the most inspiring in the history of the American Negro. Born one-eighth Negro, he had blond hair and blue eyes; and he could have "passed" as a white man if he had chosen to. Growing racial tensions in his home town of Augusta, Georgia, and the influence of two local Negro leaders led the boy to realize that his place was with the Negro. When he was eighteen, he left Augusta for Worcester, Massachusetts, where he worked his way through Worcester Academy. His fine record there and at Brown University attested to his intelligence and his industry, but most important, it strengthened his resolve to help his people by improving their education. Torrence describes Hope's ambitions after graduating from Brown: "In September, 1894, John Hope went to Nashville, Tennessee. His aim was threefold: to be in his native South again, to be among his own people, and to find out whether teaching might be his natural calling. He had come under the influence of three great teachers—George Willaims Walker in Augusta, D. W. Abercrombie in Worcester, and Benjamin Andrews at Brown—and the role seemed to him an inspired one. As for the hold the South and his race had upon him, that was subtler and deeper, a thing of the innermost heart" (106).

From this point on, Hope devoted himself to the education of the Negro. From 1894–98, he taught science at Roger Williams University in Nashville; in 1898, he was appointed professor of Classics at Atlanta Baptist College; and in 1906, he became its president, thus earning the distinction of being the first Negro president of a Baptist college. As president, Hope did all he could to raise the standards of the college; and he continued to teach logic and ethics. Hope remained president of Atlanta Baptist (later renamed Morehouse College) until 1929 when Morehouse and Spelman Colleges affiliated with Atlanta University. The objective of this merger was to allow Morehouse and Spelman to take full responsibility for undergraduate instruction so that Atlanta University could devote itself solely to graduate education. Hope was unanimously elected president of Atlanta University, the first Negro university to offer graduate degrees.

Hope did not restrict his interest in the Negro to educational matters. He campaigned actively for equality for the Negro; and, through his work with the National Association for the Advancement of Colored People, the Urban League, and the World Committee of the Young Men's Christian Association, he did much to improve the lot of his people. When he died in 1936, tributes from all parts of America and the world were offered, but few were as eloquent as that written by Torrence twelve years later:

> The house where he was born no longer stands. The tower that stood in Augusta, the silent bell, and the blind watchman who never warned of danger are long since swept away. High over their empty place and over all the nation the four quarters of the sky are coursed by the planes. From them the Negroes often look down at the land of their nativity. The land they see is veiled to their countrymen of other races. They see where they live. They live in shadows cast by none of the clouds of heaven. Fogs wall them in and roof them there below, exhalations from the depths, unbreathable mists born of darkness in the heart of man. John Hope was a dispeller of shadows, shining through them with the native radiations of his spirit and the lightnings of his never-daunted passion. Because he lived, the winds of time can a little sooner lift them away. (374)

It is unfortunate that Torrence waited until he was over seventy to write a major prose work. *The Story of John Hope* is characterized not only by a full command of the subject but also by a beautiful style that makes the work an exceptionally fine biography. As one critic has observed: "In this powerful narrative Ridgely Torrence has given us the full story of a most interesting and worthy man. The book is a product of scholarship of the highest order. But it is also more than that. It is a blending of the poet's skill and devotion with the hard facts of a noble life." [26]

The Story of John Hope was Ridgely Torrence's last published work. Shortly after Thanksgiving, 1950, he entered the Lenox Hill Hospital in New York with lung cancer, and he died on Christmas Day. There were the usual obituaries and memorials, as well as many expressions of grief from his numerous friends; but the gen-

eral public merely noticed the passing of another minor figure
from the literary scene. In terms of public recognition, Ridgely
Torrence never was a successful poet. His volumes are out of
print, and his name is known only by the official guardians of
literary memory. He deserved better.

CHAPTER 8

Assessment

> He was an admirable man and an
> under-rated poet.
>
> —Allen Tate[1]

IT is difficult to do justice to the life and career of any artist,
and often it is even more difficult to give a fair appraisal of his
work. But the question that is inevitably asked is not the simple
"What did the write?" but rather "What did he achieve?" Ridgely
Torrence was not a prolific poet, nor was he a particularly popular one. He had the respect of his colleagues and critics, but he
never gained sufficient popular acclaim to keep his name alive
after his death. Yet much of his work is very good indeed, and a
fair assessment of his strengths and weaknesses—of his achieve-
ments and failures—must either explain his obscurity or justify a
reappraisal.

For the first fifteen years of his career Torrence was a chame-
leonlike figure, adapting himself to whatever literary environ-
ment he happened to be enjoying at the time. Such eclecticism is
not uncommon in a young artist, and the ability to work com-
fortably within a popular mode can be quite profitable for a commercial writer, but poets seldom fall into the commercial category
and are more often judged by their individual traits. It took Torrence a long time to develop his own medium of communication—perhaps too long to establish his reputation, for critics and
other readers lose interest in a promising poet unless there is a
new volume every few years.

His first volume, *The House of a Hundred Lights,* cannot be
considered an important work, though the critics thought it was
promising. It is, first of all, an attempt to capitalize upon the popularity of another work, *The Rubaiyat of Omar Khayyam;* but
FitzGerald had a richer work to adapt and enough of a mastery

of Omar's language and background to capture the full flavor of the poetry. Torrence's work was not really a translation but an imitation of Bidpai's couplets in form, for the substance of the work was Torrence's own invention. Unfortunately, there is nothing at all original about Torrence's contribution to the work of Bidpai. It is eclectic, a quality which need not be negative, but the only traditions the young poet had to draw upon were dying ones—the ornate verbal arabesques of the late Victorians and the homely saws of the American fireside poets. Whitman was not "Genteel" enough for a disciple of Edmund Clarence Stedman, and to be considered a regional poet was the last thing Torrence wanted at this time. He was trapped, therefore, by influences upon him and by his own inclination, into drawing heat from the dying embers of the poetry of the generation before him.

It was fortunate for Torrence that he became associated with the leaders of the poetry of his own generation. The vigorous spirit of William Vaughn Moody and the brilliance of E. A. Robinson and Josephine Preston Peabody could not help but be positive forces in the development of his poetic talent. Moreover, they were right in believing that the voice of the American poet needed a new medium in which to express itself, and their experiments in poetic drama marked an important chapter in the history of American poetry, but they were doomed from the beginning. No clearer evidence of the futility of the verse drama movement can be found than Torrence's two verse plays, *El Dorado* and *Abelard and Heloise*. While they are not by any means bad examples of the genre, they illustrate its limitations. The characters are cardboard idealizations with conflicts and emotions that might have been suitable in a more Romantic period, but they were out of place in the America of Torrence's time. While popular taste may still have shown a taste for knights in armor and alluring but chaste nymphs, the naturalists had demonstrated vividly the need for a literature that truly reflected its own time and place. Stedman was right when he wrote Percy MacKaye, "You only show your own limitations when you profess to show yourselves unable to find American atmosphere and themes for American dramas." [2] The story of the romance between Abelard and Heloise was hardly relevant to America at the turn of the century, nor was the idealized account of Coronado's quest for gold.

America did not want elevated poetic dramas about ideal love and chivalry. It wanted to see plays about its own concerns, whether they were presented as pure melodrama, such as David Belasco's *The Girl of the Golden West;* as comedy, such as Langdon Mitchell's *The New York Idea;* or as a problem play such as Moody's *The Great Divide.* Of course, the artificiality of the characters and situations in Torrence's poetic dramas is partly a result of the awkwardness of blank verse as the medium for a distinctly American play. It was the natural tool for an artist working in Elizabethan England and writing about kings and nobles, but America offered no such elevated figures. Even Shakespeare, for whom blank verse was a natural and convenient device, used prose for his more mundane characters and actions. Torrence's verse in these plays is good but at times seems strained and archaic.

It did not take long for Moody and his colleagues to realize that poetry would not be the medium for American drama and that a play could be poetic without limiting itself to outmoded and irrelevant forms. Inspired by Moody's success with *The Great Divide,* Torrence turned his attention to the writing of plays in prose. While these are clearly transitional works, the changes in material and style that he introduced are crucial ones. First, these plays are closer to Torrence's own experiences, for the action takes place in Torrence's own area of Ohio, and the plays are based in part on the folklore of this region. Their language, however, is highly metaphorical and often stilted—obviously the work of a novice. The plays, never published or produced, are not successful artistically, possibly because they are too ambitious in scope. Torrence had a good deal of talent; but he was yet to realize that, like Frost, his best work would be on a small scale.

His work in the next decade would not only prove his mastery of the short lyric and the one-act play but would also mark the high point of his career. His Negro plays—*Granny Maumee, The Rider of Dreams,* and *Simon the Cyrenian*—are admirable. The simple, natural, yet lyrical language is a perfect medium for the characters and situations; and the dialogue demonstrates Torrence's fine ear for the nuances of speech of the people with whom he was familiar. As a matter of fact, the language of the plays distinguishes them more than any ideas they might convey.

Granny Maumee shows a mastery of theatrical effect, but the play is more melodrama than tragedy. Its crucial scene is dependent on an impossible coincidence, and Granny's final hallucination does not quite ring true. *Simon the Cyrenian,* the only one of the plays in verse, is more powerful. Here Torrence has a moral to convey, "Those who live by the sword shall perish by the sword," and has incorporated it in an eloquent little play. Again, there is too much coincidence, but this matters less in a nonrealistic framework.

The Rider of Dreams is the best of the plays because of its delightful title character, Madison Sparrow. While Sparrow is something of an archetype, Torrence has succeeded in making him a convincingly three-dimensional character. As with the other two plays, the plot hangs upon some absurd improbabilities, and here we have hit upon Torrence's weakness as a dramatist: he could create interesting characters and write fine dialogue for them; he could manipulate dramatic image and symbol with ease; but he could not devise a coherent, probable plot. This weakness plagued his earlier three-act prose plays and his poetic dramas, and is evident in the Negro works. The plays are technically superb, but the technique covers a slight framework. Whatever their flaws, however, Torrence's Negro plays were crucial to the history of the American theater. The experience of the American Negro was a perfect subject for dramatic treatment, and in this area Torrence was years ahead of his time.

The area in which Torrence distinguished himself was the short lyric, and the poetry he wrote between 1915 and 1925 shows a mastery of the form. There is no doubt that Torrence was wise in restricting himself to a form in which he excelled and in writing only about those things that concerned him most deeply. The range of subjects is limited—for the most part, the poems are expressions of Torrence's faith in the human spirit as the source of all fulfillment, or of his loathing of cruelty and injustice, whether manifested in war or in racial prejudice. The poem's theme is often projected through the use of some sort of vision; but, rather than present an ideal situation, the vision usually leads the poet back to himself as the source of happiness or fulfillment.

These poems are often simple in structure, but they are complex in meter. Torrence was fond of using a dactyllic or anapestic line punctuated by a spondee or an iamb. The use of these three-syllable feet produced a long line with relatively few strongly stressed syllables. The extremely simple language of the poems is limited usually to one- and two-syllable words, but the poems abound in long vowel sounds. The combination of this simple language with its many long vowels and its complex meter gives Torrence's line a fluidity, a smoothness, and a gravity of tone. For these lyrics which demonstrate complete mastery of a simple, yet highly disciplined form, Torrence deserves a high place in American poetry. Unlike his earlier works, the poems collected in *Hesperides* are in no way "dated." They are distinctive and their idiom is Torrence's own.

After a ten-year silence, Torrence began writing again, and his later poems show the same technical mastery as those of the previous decade. It is a sad fact that his later and best poems are contained within a mere hundred and forty pages. Perhaps the small number of these poems accounts for their present obscurity. Few American poets have been able to sustain a reputation on such a small body of work. There is, however, an inescapable factor that we confront in assessing these poems. While they are all good, there is a sameness that we cannot help but notice in reading a volume of Torrence's poetry. This is not due to the technique. There is enough variety of language, meter, and rhyme scheme to satisfy any but the most demanding critic. Rather it comes from the weakness that beset Torrence from the beginning of his literary career. He was a fine craftsman, but he was limited in subject matter and themes. Possibly this paucity of poetic "ideas" explains the long "dry" periods when the poet produced nothing. Stedman, concerned about this weakness in the early years of the century, warned Torrence about it: "Now that your *expression* is so fully at your command, wreak it [exertion] upon your thought—i.e., reverse the process attributed to him who 'wreaked his thoughts upon expression.' Do so, my dear Ridgely, even though this preachment is that of a lessening oracle, and you will be a bard indeed, and put an end to the foolish plaint that Poetry can be of worth no more." [3]

Application and exertion seldom replace inspiration as the source of poetic excellence, at least so far as the kind of poetry Torrence wished to write is concerned. Such contemporaries as Eliot, Tate, and Pound postulated that inspiration was not a prime requisite for poetry; but Torrence was not a "modern" in this sense, and the fact that his poems repeat themselves is distressing, especially as they were written over a period of twenty-five years. Torrence was essentially a fine craftsman, seldom an inspired poet.

The quarter century in which he produced his best work was a remarkable period of innovation in American poetry. During the years in which he was writing the poems that comprised the *Hesperides* volume, the American Imagists were sounding their battle cry in London and Chicago; Eliot wrote *The Waste Land* with the help of Ezra Pound who had begun his *Cantos;* Sandburg, Vachel Lindsay, and Edgar Lee Masters were experimenting within the area of regional poetry; and Wallace Stevens wrote *Harmonium.* None of this work seems to have affected Torrence, which is especially surprising in light of his role as poetry editor of *The New Republic.* He read the work of these poets and even accepted some of it for publication, but he did not assimilate their advances into his own work. But we do not indicate that Torrence was the only conservative: Frost was never an innovator, nor was Robinson, whose later work was repetitious and regressive. Still, it is astonishing that Torrence did not respond to the exciting new poets, considering his earlier eagerness to try new forms.

We cannot do justice to Torrence's career without acknowledging his devoted service to the cause of American letters. As poetry editor of *The New Republic,* he was influential in offering a platform to many gifted young poets and was also responsible for setting a high standard of quality for the magazine's poetry. As a founding member of the Academy of American Poets, Torrence raised the funds to aid many of our country's most talented literary artists. In addition, he helped to raise the prestige of the American poet to that of a respected voice in our society. His promotional material for the Academy of American Poets makes it clear that he felt that a society should help to support its poets. The fellowships awarded each year by the academy mark an important step in this direction. Torrence's concern for, and service to, the American Negro have been discussed elsewhere.

Ridgely Torrence did not come of age as an artist until he was nearly forty years old, but his work after this time is not without flaws. He did not have the keen, probing intellect of an

Eliot or a Pound, the fanciful imagination of a Stevens, or the wit of a Frost. He did have a mastery of poetic technique, however, that surpassed that of many of his more "original" colleagues. Because of his skill with the tools of the poet, Torrence in his later work is seldom less than a good poet. This, it seems to me, is saying quite enough. It is doubtful that Torrence will ever emerge from obscurity and attain a high position in American literature, but his work merits consideration, and his service to his vocation is worthy of tribute. At least the *Hesperides* poems deserve to be known and remembered by anyone truly interested in the American literary tradition.

Notes and References

Chapter One

1. Ridgely Torrence, "Country Bred in New York," *Greene County: 1803–1908* (Xenia, 1908), p. 1. The volume is a belated centennial tribute to Greene County; and contains contributions from a number of local authors.

2. From the typescript of an unfinished autobigraphy which Torrence entitled "Reminiscences." From the Ridgely Torrence papers, Princeton University Library.

3. "Reminiscences."

4. Letter to Robert S. Newdick, October 12, 1936. This and all other letters cited, unless otherwise noted, are from the Ridgely Torrence Papers, Princeton University Library. In the fall of 1935 Newdick, a student at Miami when Torrence taught there (1920–21) and at this time an assistant professor at Ohio State University, wrote Torrence and asked for permission to do a complete bibliography of his works as well as for Torrence's cooperation on the subject. The bibliography never reached completion as Newdick died in 1939 before completing the critical biography that was to accompany the bibliography.

5. "Reminiscences."

6. *Ibid.*

7. Letter from R. T. to his mother, January 12, 1895.

8. Letter from R. T. to his mother, November 8, 1894.

9. Letter from R. T. to his mother, February 14, 1895.

10. Letter from R. T. to his mother, November 8, 1894.

11. Ridgely Torrence, "A Japanese Girl," *The Miami Student* (May, 1897).

12. Written by Torrence's father on envelope in which he kept his son's poems.

13. Letter from R. T. to his father, September 25, 1895.

14. *Bric-a-Brac* (The Princeton Yearbook, 1898), p. 166.

15. Ridgely Torrence, "Silenus," *The Nassau Literary Magazine* LI (January, 1896), 348.

16. Ridgely Torrence, "Receipt for a Song," *The Nassau Literary Magazine,* LI (February, 1896), 421.

17. Letter from R. T. to his father, April 1, 1896.

18. Letter from R. T. to his mother, April 6, 1896.

19. Letter from R. T. to his father, December 15, 1896.

20. Letter from R. T. to his father (undated, but probably early 1897).

21. Letter from R. T. to his parents, April 4, 1897.

22. Letter from R. T. to his parents, April 23, 1897.

23. Letter from R. T. to his parents, June 20, 1897.

24. Letter from R. T. to his parents, August 12, 1897.

25. Ridgely Torrence, "Astarte," *New England Magazine* (August, 1897), p. 707.

26. Edmund Clarence Stedman, "The Hillside Door," *The Poetical Works of Edmund Clarence Stedman* (Boston, 1892), pp. 259–60.

27. Letter from R. T. to his parents, December 5, 1897.

28. Letter from R. T. to his parents, April 10, 1898.

29. Manuscript in the Ridgely Torrence Papers, Princeton University Library.

30. Manuscript in the Ridgely Torrence Papers, Princeton University Library. A Bacchic derives from the Greek religious songs to Bacchus. There is no set form of this name, although there is the bacchius, or bacchiac, a foot containing one short and two long syllables.

31. Manuscripts in the Ridgely Torrence Papers, Princeton University Library.

32. Letter from R. T. to his parents, March 3, 1898.

33. Letter to R. T. from his father, June 13, 1898.

34. Letter from R. T. to his father, June 15, 1898.

35. Letter from R. T. to his parents, October 22, 1898.

36. Manuscript in the Ridgely Torrence Papers, Princeton University Library.

37. Letter to R. T. from his father, March 2, 1899.

38. *Dictionary of American Biography,* Vol. XVII, p. 533.

39. Letter from R. T. to his parents, March 25, 1899.

40. Letter from R. T. to his parents, March 27, 1899.

41. Letter from R. T. to his parents, June 2, 1899.

42. Letter from R. T. to his parents, September 29, 1899.

43. *The House of a Hundred Lights* (Boston, 1899). All subsequent quotes are from this edition. The volume's pages are unnumbered.

44. Booth Tarkington, Review of *The House of a Hundred Lights,* Indianapolis *Press,* February 3, 1900.

45. Anon. review of *The House of a Hundred Lights*, New York *Tribune*, March 10, 1910.

46. Anon. review of *The House of a Hundred Lights, The Critic*, XXXIV (August, 1900), 184.

47. John Greenleaf Whittier, "What the Voice Said," *Poems* (Boston, 1850), p. 319.

48. John B. Tabb, "Prejudice," *Poems* (Boston, 1894), p. 128.

49. Bliss Carman (with Richard Hovey), "Hem and Haw," *More Songs From Vagabondia* (Boston, 1896), p. 70.

Chapter Two

1. Letter from Zona Gale to R. T., undated but probably 1924.

2. *El Dorado, A Tragedy* (London & New York, 1903), "Prologue."

3. Edmund Clarence Stedman, ed., *An American Anthology, 1787–1900* (New York, 1900). Torrence's contributions are on pages 752–753.

4. Letter from R. T. to Josephine Preston Peabody, May 29, 1900.

5. Hermann Hagedorn, *Edwin Arlington Robinson: A Biography* (New York, 1938), pp. 164–65.

6. Manuscript in the Ridgely Torrence Papers, Princeton University Library.

7. Letter from R. T. to his parents, June 8, 1900.

8. A. G. Lehmann, *The Symbolist Movement in France, 1885–1895* (Oxford, 1950), p. 207.

9. Letter from R. T. to his parents, June 8, 1900.

10. Letter from R. T. to his parents, April 15, 1900.

11. Letter from R. T. to his parents, April 29, 1900.

12. *Ibid.*

13. Letter from R. T. to Josephine Preston Peabody, August 27, 1900.

14. Josephine Preston Peabody, *Marlowe* (Cambridge, Mass., 1901).

15. Quoted in Arthur Hobson Quinn, *A History of American Drama from the Civil War to the Present Day* (New York, 1937), III, 11.

16. Letter from Edwin Arlington Robinson to R. T., November 2, 1900. Early in 1907, Robinson wrote two plays; *Van Zorn*, a story of a love triangle; *The Porcupine*, a study of New England village life. Neither was produced, but both were eventually published: *Van Zorn*, 1914; *The Porcupine*, 1915.

17. Letter from R. T. to Josephine Preston Peabody, August 27, 1900.

18. Letter from R. T. to his parents, November 15, 1901.

19. Letter from R. T. to his parents, February 3, 1902.

20. Letter from R. T. to his parents, January 26, 1902.

21. Letter from R. T. to his parents, February 23, 1902.

22. Ridgely Torrence, "The Entreaty," *The Smart Set*, VIII (October, 1902).

23. Letter from R. T. to his parents, December 27, 1901.

24. Letter from R. T. to his parents, July 16, 1902.

25. Zona Gale, "You," *The Smart Set*, February, 1903, p. 21.

26. Letter from R. T. to his parents, November 25, 1902.

27. Letter from R. T. to his parents, December 2, 1902.

28. Letter from his mother to R. T., August 19, 1902.

29. Letter from R. T. to his parents, June 4, 1904.

30. Letter from Zona Gale to R. T., September 29, 1904.

31. *Ibid.* Zona's reaction to her romance with Torrence and its unhappy ending is well presented in Peter Simonson's study, *Zona Gale* (New York, 1962), pp. 26–31.

32. Letter from R. T. to his parents, March 9, 1903.

33. Letter from R. T. to his parents, May 2, 1904.

34. Letter from R. T. to Laura Stedman, September 18, 1900.

35. *Ibid.*

36. *El Dorado: A Tragedy* (New York and London, 1903), p. 104. All references are to this edition.

37. Lyman Leathers, "Ridgely Torrence and the Search for an American Identity," (Univ. of Pennsylvania, 1963), p. 95.

38. "H. C., review of *El Dorado, The Reader*, February, 1904.

39. Anon. review of *El Dorado*, the New York *Post*, November 12, 1903.

40. Guy Carleton Lee, review of *El Dorado*, Los Angeles *Times*, October 17, 1903.

41. Edith M. Thomas, review of *El Dorado, The Critic*, XLIII (December, 1903), 567.

Chapter Three

1. William Vaughn Moody, *Letters to Harriet*, ed. Percy MacKaye (Boston, 1935), p. 172.

2. "Verse—Recent and Old," *The Critic*, XLV (August, 1904), 152.

3. "The Masque of Hours," *The Critic*, XLV (March, 1904), 258–260.

4. These opinions of R. T.'s work on *The Critic* are taken from Robert S. Newdick's notes for a biography of Torrence. The notes are records of conversations with Torrence that the scholar had made before his death in 1939.

5. *Selected Letters of Edwin Arlington Robinson,* ed. Ridgely Torrence (New York, 1940), pp. 52–53.

6. "An Inscription," reprinted in *The Greene County Historical Society Bulletin,* No. 6 (December, 1957).

7. Letter from R. T. to his parents, March 15, 1905.

8. *Selected Letters of Edwin Arlington Robinson,* p. 62.

9. Letter from Edwin Arlington Robinson to Josephine Preston Peabody, September 9, 1905. Ridgely Torrence Papers, Princeton University Library.

10. "Mr. Torrence's Metrical Art," *The Atlantic Monthly,* XCVI (November, 1905), 712.

11. *Ibid.,* p. 714.

12. *Ibid.,* p. 715.

13. "The Lesser Children: A Threnody at the Hunting Season," *The Atlantic Monthly,* XCVI (September, 1905), 326–27.

14. *Ibid.,* p. 327.

15. Letter from R. T. to his parents, May 12, 1906.

16. May Sinclair, "Three American Poets of Today," *Fortnightly Review,* LXXXVI (September 1, 1906), 422.

17. *Ibid.,* pp. 424–25.

18. *Ibid.,* p. 431.

19. *Ibid.,* p. 435.

20. Letter from R. T. to his parents, May 25, 1906.

21. Letter from R. T. to his parents, May 18, 1906.

22. Hermann Hagedorn, *Edwin Arlington Robinson: A Biography* (New York, 1938), pp. 225–26.

23. Letter from R. T. to his brother, Findley, January 11, 1907. Findley, then a student at Harvard, was writing a term paper on E. A. R. and asked his brother for some insights.

24. Letter from R. T. to his parents, January 19, 1906.

25. Daniel Gregory Mason, *Music in My Time and Other Reminiscences* (New York, 1938), pp. 140–42.

26. Jeannette L. Gilder, review of *Abelard and Heloise,* Boston *Evening Transcript,* March 13, 1907.

27. Anon. review, *Abelard and Heloise, The Book Buyer* (March, 1907).

28. W. S. Braithwaite, review of *Abelard and Heloise,* Boston *Evening Transcript,* March 13, 1907.

29. *Abelard and Heloise* (New York, 1907), p. 43. All citations are from this edition.

30. Letter to Ridgely Torrence. Quoted in Laura Stedman (Gould), *Edmund Clarence Stedman: His Life and Letters* (New York, 1910), II, pp. 118–19.

Chapter Four

1. William Vaughn Moody, *Letters to Harriet,* ed. Percy MacKaye (Boston, 1935), p. 319.

2. William Morton Payne, "The Poetry of Mr. Moody," *The Dial* (December 16, 1912), p. 485.

3. Quoted in David D. Henry, *William Vaughn Moody* (Boston, 1914), p. 171.

4. Letter from R. T. to his parents, October 13, 1906.

5. Letter from R. T. to his parents, January 12, 1907.

6. *Ibid.*

7. Letter from R. T. to his parents, January 17, 1907.

8. Letter from R. T. to his parents, February 2, 1907.

9. This and all subsequent references to *The Madstone* are from an unpublished typescript of the play in the Ridgely Torrence Papers, Princeton University Library.

10. Letter from R. T. to his parents, January 12, 1800.

11. Draft of a letter, Ridgely Torrence Papers, Princeton University Library.

12. *Letters to Harriet,* p. 330.

13. Letter from R. T. to his parents, April 16, 1907.

14. Letter from R. T. to his parents, May 3, 1907.

15. This and all subsequent references to *The Thunder Pool* are from an unpublished manuscript of the play, Ridgely Torrence Papers, Princeton University Library.

16. Letter from R. T. to his parents, January 2, 1908.

17. Letter from R. T. to his parents, March 27, 1908.

18. Letter from R. T. to William Vaughn Moody, August 31, 1907.

19. Letter from R. T. to his parents, May 12, 1909.

20. Letter from R. T. to William Vaughn Moody, May 29, 1906.

21. Letter from R. T. to William Vaughn Moody, February 17, 1909.

22. Letter from R. T. to his parents, December 23, 1907.

23. Letter from R. T. to his parents, January 27, 1901.

24. "Ritual for the Body's Passing," *Hesperides* (New York, 1925), p. 105.

25. "Ritual for Birth and Naming," *The Century Magazine,* LXXVIII (September, 1909), 728–30.

26. Letter from R. T. to his brother, July 23, 1911; Torrence was probably led to this movement by Harriet Moody, who was zealous in her belief in Mental Science. Thomas Troward, a former divisional judge at Punjab, was one of Britain's foremost spokesmen for Mental

Science. His *Edinburgh Lectures on Mental Science* (1909) was one of the most influential books on a religion which believed that "the intellect becomes the handmaid of that interior power within us which manipulates the unseen substance of all things." Thomas Troward, *Edinburgh Lectures on Mental Science* (New York, 1915), p. 62.

27. Ridgely Torrence, "Three O'Clock," *Scribner's Magazine*, XLIV (December, 1908), 760.

28. Letter from R. T. to William Vaughn Moody, August 31, 1907.

29. Letter from R. T. to Daniel Gregory Mason, October 22, 1910.

30. Ridgely Torrence, "Santa Barbara Beach," *Poetry: A Magazine of Verse*, I (March, 1913), 180–81.

Chapter Five

1. Letter from R. T. to W. O. Walker, editor of Cleveland *Call Post*, January, 1939.

2. Telegram from R. T. to his parents, February 3, 1914.

3. Letter from Edwin Arlington Robinson to R. T., February 9, 1914.

4. Chard Powers Smith, *Where the Light Falls; A Portrait of Edwin Arlington Robinson* (New York, 1965), p. 239. Smith seems to find the idea of an affair between E. A. R. and Olivia Dunbar doubtful (see note, p. 404).

5. Letter from R. T. to Harriet Moody, May 5, 1915.

6. Edith J. R. Isaacs, *The Negro in the American Theatre* (New York, 1947), p. 60.

7. Edward Sheldon, *The Nigger* (New York, 1910), p. 245. The play was first performed December 4, 1909.

8. "The New Negro Theater," *The Crisis: A Record of the Darker Races*, XIV (June, 1917), 80.

9. From typescript of unpublished memoir, Ridgely Torrence Papers, Princeton University Library.

10. *Ibid.*

11. Letter from R. T. to Harriet Moody, February, 1914.

12. Carl Van Vechten, review *Granny Maumee*, New York *Press*, March 31, 1914.

13. Anon. review *Granny Maumee*, Rochester *Evening Times*, May 19, 1914.

14. Letter from R. T. to his parents, May 1, 1915.

15. Hermann Hagedorn, *Edwin Arlington Robinson: A Biography* (New York, 1938), p. 295.

16. Letter from R. T. to his family, February 2, 1917.

17. Letter from R. T. to his family, February 23, 1917.

18. Letter from R. T. to his family, March 2, 1917.

19. Letter from R. T. to Harriet Moody, March 12, 1917.

20. Robert C. Benchley, "Can This Be the Native American Drama?," New York *Tribune*, April 1, 1917, pt. 5, p. 6.

21. Francis Hackett, "After the Play" (review Negro Plays), *The New Republic*, XI (April 14, 1917), 325.

22. Alexander Woolcott, "The Colored Players," *The New York Times*, April 29, 1917, sec. 8, p. 7.

23. Letter from R. T. to his family, April 20, 1917.

24. Randolph Bourne, Letter to the Editor of *New York Tribune*, April 10, 1917, p. 10.

25. Ridgely Torrence, *Granny Maumee, The Rider of Dreams, Simon the Cyrenian: Plays for a Negro Theatre* (New York, 1917). All citations will be from this text.

Chapter Six

1. Robert Frost, "A Passing Glimpse," *West-running Brook* (New York, 1928), p. 13.

2. "A Vision of Spring," *The New Republic*, II (March 20, 1915), 180–81. Published in later volumes as "The Winter Crystal."

3. "The Bird and the Tree," *Poetry: A Magazine of Verse*, VI (April, 1915), 20–21.

4. "I Will Send the Comforter," *The New Republic*, VI (February 26, 1916), 106. Published in later volumes in a shortened version entitled "Headland Orchards."

5. Letter from R. T. to Harriet Moody, August 17, 1916.

6. Alfred Tennyson, "Hesperides," from *Poetical Works* (Oxford, 1953), p. 847.

7. Louis Untermeyer, "Achievement," (review *Hesperides*), *The Saturday Review of Literature*, I (May 16, 1925), 756.

8. "The Son," *The New Republic*, VI (February 26, 1916), 107.

9. "Eye Witness," *Scribner's Magazine*, LX (December 16, 1916), 653–57.

10. Daniel Gregory Mason, *Music in My Time and Other Reminiscences* (New York, 1938), p. 145.

11. Ridgely Torrence, "Survivors," *Poetry: A Magazine of Verse*, IX (January, 1917), 188.

12. Letter from R. T. to his family, May 4; 1917. Torrence's feelings about pacifism did not abate after the war. In 1937, he expressed his feelings about it in an interview for the Columbus *Dispatch*: "If I am anything, I am a war resister, and to the old question of 'What would you do if a blood thirsty maniac entered your home and attacked your small child,' I answer, as Emerson did 85 years ago, 'Nature will tell me what to do in that suppositious hour. Meanwhile I will not

base my philosophy on the faint possibility of a maniac's demeanor.' "
Columbus *Dispatch*, March 9, 1937, p. 14A.

13. Letter from R. T. to Harriet Moody, June 12, 1917.

14. "Sea Dream," *The New Republic*, XIII (November 10, 1917), 51.

15. "Peace," The Boston *Transcript*, November 23, 1918, pt. 3, p. 4.

16. "To Children: Invitation, Jean Singing," *The New Republic*, XVII (December 28, 1918), 251.

17. "The Apples," *The Nation*, CX (March 3, 1920), 854. Published in later volumes under the title, "Legend."

18. Ridgely Torrence, "The Feasters," *The Nation*, CXI (July 24, 1920), 102.

19. Letter from Carl Sandburg to R. T., September 27, 1920.

20. Ridgely Torrence, "The Singers in a Cloud," *The Dial*, LXIX (November, 1920), 489.

21. Letter from R. T. to Harriet Moody, March 4, 1919.

22. Letter from Robert Frost to Harriet Moody, April 21, 1919, *Selected Letters of Robert Frost*, ed. Lawrance Thompson (New York, 1964), p. 237.

23. Letter from R. T. to Harriet Moody, December 1, 1915.

24. Letter from Robert Frost to Harriet Moody, January, 1923, quoted in Olivia Dunbar, *A House in Chicago* (Chicago, 1947), p. 193.

25. "Hesperides," *Hesperides* (New York, 1925), pp. 9–17. This poem appears in later editions as "The Apples." The earlier poem entitled "The Apples" becomes "Legend."

26. Louis Untermeyer, "Achievement" (review *Hesperides*), *The Saturday Review of Literature*, I (May 16, 1925), 756.

Chapter Seven

1. Letter from Malcolm Cowley to John M. Clum, July 23, 1966.

2. Quoted in The New York *Herald*, Paris edition, August 9, 1925, p. 10.

3. Letter from Carrie Clive Bliss to Bruce Bliven, October 18, 1932. Ridgely Torrencee Papers, Princeton University Library.

4. Letter from Bruce Bliven to John M. Clum, July 14, 1966.

5. Letter from Malcolm Cowley to John M. Clum, July 23, 1966.

6. Rolf Humphries, review *Poems by Ridgely Torrence*, *The New Republic* CIX (October 27, 1941), 565.

7. Letter from Bruce Bliven to John M. Clum, July 14, 1966.

8. Chard Powers Smith, *Where the Light Falls: A Biography of Edwin Arlington Robinson* (New York, 1965), p. 366.

9. Introduction, *Selected Letters of Edwin Arlington Robinson* (New York, 1940), p. viii.

10. *Ibid.,* p. vii.

11. Letter from R. T. to Robert S. Newdick, December 7, 1936.

12. "Outline," *Saturday Review of Literature,* XIV (May 30, 1936), 6.

13. Quoted in "A History of the Academy of American Poets" (promotional brochure) (New York, 1966).

14. "Europa and the Bull," *The New Republic,* XCI (May 5, 1937), 379.

15. "Men and Wheat," *The New Republic,* XCI (May 26, 1937), 72.

16. "On Storm King Edge," *The New Republic,* XCVIII (June 7, 1939), 99.

17. "Notes on the Negro Theatre," unpublished report to the Rockefeller Foundation, 1939. Copy in Ridgely Torrence Papers, Princeton University Library.

18. "Five Poems," *Poetry: A Magazine of Verse,* LV (November, 1939), 59–65.

19. "Lincoln's Dream," *The New Republic,* CVI (February 10, 1941), 171–72. "Yes there is data for the poem. I am surprised that you don't know it. Lincoln often had a dream of being on a ship. He dreamed it again on the night before his death and mentioned it at cabinet meeting that afternoon not long before he went to the theatre. He also dreamed, a short time before, of seeing himself lying dead in the East Room of the White House, where his body actually did lie a short time later. And he did see his double image in the glass in Springfield. Of course these things are recorded in a few meagre sentences from the reports of persons to whom he told these things but they are on record. Lincoln was a visionary. He lived in both worlds, sleeping and waking, in spite of being a monument of horse sense. He was a seer and visionary of the same kind (though not in the same degree) that Swedenborg and Blake were." Draft of letter to Paula Jakobi (1941).

20. *Poems, by Ridgely Torrence* (New York, 1941), p. 40. Subsequent page references are to this volume.

21. Rolf Humphries, review *Poems, by Ridgely Torrence, The New Republic,* CIX (October 27, 1941), 564–65.

22. Louis Untermeyer, "Richness and Restraint," *The Saturday Review of Literature,* XXIV (July 19, 1941), 6.

23. *Poems, by Ridgely Torrence* (New York, 1952).

24. Ridgely Torrence, "Ygdrasil," *The Saturday Review of Literature,* XXIX (September 7, 1946), 12.

25. *The Story of John Hope* (New York, 1948).

26. Rufus Early Clement, "Hard Facts of a Noble Life," (review *The Story of John Hope*), *The Saturday Review of Literature*, XXXI (August 7, 1948), 24.

Chapter Eight

1. Letter from Allen Tate to John M. Clum, June 30, 1966.

2. Quoted in Laura Stedman (Gould), *The Life and Letters of Edmund Clarence Stedman*, 2 vols. (New York, 1910), II, 118–19.

3. Letter from E. C. Stedman to Ridgely Torrence, September 7, 1905.

Selected Bibliography

PRIMARY SOURCES

Entries are presented in chronological order, but magazine verse will be listed separately only if not published in one of the later volumes.

"Silenus," *The Nassau Literary Magazine*, LI (January, 1896), 348.
"Receipt for a Song," *The Nassau Literary Magazine*, LI (February, 1896), 421.
"The Owl," *The Nassau Literary Magazine*, LII (May, 1896), 1–2.
"A Memory," *The Nassau Literary Magazine*, LII (June, 1896), 84.
"A Japanese Girl," *The Miami Student*, (April, 1897), p. 113.
"Astarte (after seeing Sargent's fresco in the Boston Library)," *New England Magazine*, XVII (August, 1897), 707.
The House of a Hundred Lights. Boston: Small, Maynard and Company, 1899.
"The Entreaty," *The Smart Set*, VIII (October, 1902), 101.
El Dorado: A Tragedy. New York and London: John Lane, 1903.
"The Masque of Hours," *The Critic*, XLIV (March, 1904), 258–60.
"Verse—Recent and Old," *The Critic*, XLV (August, 1904), 151–56.
Abelard and Heloise. New York: Charles Scribner's Sons, 1907.
"Country Bred. In New York," *Greene County: 1803–1908*. Xenia, Ohio, 1908, p. 1.
"Ritual for a Marriage," *The Century Magazine*, LXXVIII (August, 1909), 516–18.
Granny Maumee, The Rider of Dreams, Simon the Cyrenian: Plays for a Negro Theatre. New York: The Macmillan Company, 1917.
"Danse Calinda: A Pantomine with Folk Music," *Theatre Arts Magazine*, III (July, 1919), 204–12.
Hesperides. New York: The Macmillan Company, 1925.
The Story of Gio (Children's book) New York: Japan Society, 1935.
(Editor) *Selected Letters of Edwin Arlington Robinson*. New York: The Macmillan Company, 1941.
Poems, by Ridgely Torrence. New York: The Macmillan Company, 1941.

(Editor) *The Last Poems of Anna Hempstead Branch*. New York: Farrar and Rinehart, Inc., 1944.
The Story of John Hope. New York: The Macmillan Company, 1948.
Poems, by Ridgely Torrence. New York: The Macmillan Company, 1952.

SECONDARY SOURCES

There has been no full-length study of Torrence, and most of the criticism is in the form of book reviews which are discussed in the text of this book. The following are volumes and articles that offer useful material on Torrence's career.

CLUM, JOHN. "Ridgely Torrence's Negro Plays: A Noble Beginning," *South Atlantic Quarterly*, LXVIII (Winter, 1969), 96–108.

DUNBAR (TORRENCE), OLIVIA. *A House in Chicago*. Chicago: University of Chicago Press, 1947. Memoir of the activities of Harriet Moody, written by Torrence's wife; offers a good deal of information about Torrence's literary associations.

HAGEDORN, HERMANN. *Edwin Arlington Robinson*. New York: The Macmillan Company, 1938. Hagedorn knew Torrence well; offers insights into Torrence's personality.

HENRY, DAVID D. *William Vaughn Moody*. Boston: Houghton Mifflin and Company, 1934. Offers some useful information about Moody's close association with Torrence.

ISAACS, EDITH J. R. *The Negro in the American Theatre*. New York: Theatre Arts Books, 1947. Devotes much attention to Torrence's plays.

LEATHERS, LYMAN LEE. "Ridgely Torrence and the Search for an American Identity," unpublished doctoral dissertation (University of Pennsylvania, 1963). Leathers describes his study as "a study of American Civilization as seen through the eyes of a particular individual during the period, 1898–1918." Torrence is seen as a man trying to adapt his nineteenth-century upbringing to the new intellectual, moral, and spiritual realities of the twentieth century. Leathers' dissertation might be termed something of a "spiritual biography" with discussions of the works as they relate to Torrence's personal concerns.

MASON, DANIEL GREGORY. *Music in My Time and Other Reminiscences*. New York: The Macmillan Company, 1938. Mason devotes a chapter to his friend Torrence.

MOODY, WILLIAM VAUGHN. *Letters to Harriet*. Ed. Percy MacKaye. Boston: Houghton Mifflin and Company, 1935. Contains many references to Torrence.

[GALE, ZONA] "Mr. Torrence's Metrical Art," *The Atlantic,* XCVIII (September, 1906), 325–35.

RITTENHOUSE, JESSIE B. *The Younger American Poets.* Boston: Little, Brown and Company, 1904. Chapter on Torrence's early work and his "promise."

SINCLAIR, MAY. "Three American Poets of Today," *Fortnightly Review,* LXXXVI (September, 1906), 421–37, reprinted in *The Atlantic,* XCVIII (September, 1906), 325–35. Discusses Moody, Robinson, and Torrence.

SMITH, CHARD POWERS. *Where the Light Falls: A Portrait of Edwin Arlington Robinson.* New York: The Macmillan Company, 1965. Memoir of Robinson contains some new information about Torrence and his friendship with the Maine poet.

Index